RON

The L. Ron Hubbard Series

BRIDGE PUBLICATIONS, INC.
5600 E. Olympic Blvd.
Commerce, California 90022 USA

ISBN 978-1-4031-9893-8

Special acknowledgment is made to the L. Ron Hubbard Library for permission to reproduce photographs from his personal collection. Additional credits: pp. 1, 9, 25, 53, 65, 83, 107, back cover Makhnach/Shutterstock.com; p. 1 © San Diego Historical Society; p. 11 Richard Thornton/Shutterstock.com; pp. 18, 42 & 43 National Archives; pp. 37–40 Frescomovie/Shutterstock.com; pp. 43–49, 93–100, 102 Tatiana53/Shutterstock.com; pp. 58 & 59 © San Diego Historical Society; pp. 67–69, 72–74, 84, 85 R-studio/Shutterstock.com; pp. 80 & 81, 91 Naval History and Heritage Command; p. 97 © Detroit Publishing Co.; p. 99 Library of Congress, Prints & Photographs Division, FSA/OWI Collection, LC-USF33-021314-M5; p. 101 Alexkar08/Shutterstock.com; pp. 104 & 105 Joe Ferrer/Shutterstock.com.

Printed in the United States of America

The L. Ron Hubbard Series: Early Years of Adventure—English

The L. Ron Hubbard Series

EARLY YEARS OF
ADVENTURE
LETTERS &
JOURNALS

Bridge

PUBLICATIONS, INC.®

CONTENTS

THE UNITED STATES

bbard

SAN JUAN
DEC 12
5=AM
1932
A-MAIL

UNITED STATES POSTAGE
10
SWELSTINE ANDREA TIEMPO

As we had been
unsuccessful in
ridding ourselves
of the boats
crew, it would
be all right: we

He stops

the beach we
went until
we came to a

Sea
ght wel

ted Sta
en from
dering
scared
ed, ner

home a
P.M.
Then dot
the headphon
and hid them
she would
denial from pie
ather.
As we
unsucces
dding nu
the boat
ew, it
all r

stop

bea

46

worth over $5,000,000 a
furnished with guards,
and servants paid. $5,00
would have been about
$4,000,000 too much. 7
boat a haywire contrap
with stone rudders an
side wheels and capsta
never cost over $15,000 a
furnished. (It is now jue
a tea pavilion.) What hap
to the rest of the money?
bled the taxpayers ou
fooled here courtie
rest of the money
is very

A pity that a ship should go to piec
For, as the boat group commander and I often
should so many try to get away when on
And so many men being brought back, w
missing men, and officers await
ports, and that usual "friend

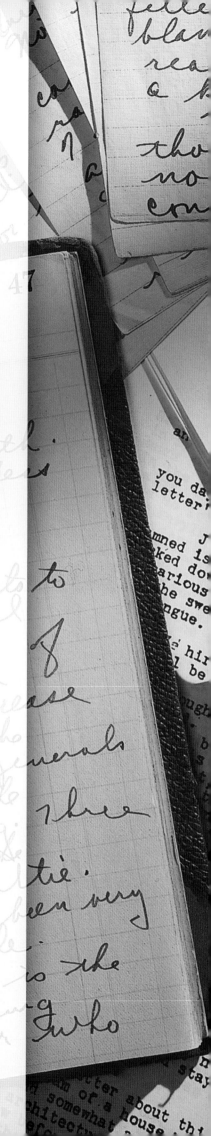

An Introductory Note

From the greater treasury of L. Ron Hubbard Archives comes a highly illuminating collection of personal letters and autobiographical journals. All told, these materials span the whole of L. Ron Hubbard's life—from his first extraordinary steps of adventure and discovery to his ultimate triumph with the founding of Dianetics and Scientology. Accordingly (and albeit representing but a fraction of his archival material) these papers provide exquisite depth and color to a most extraordinary life. Hence this special, supplemental edition within the larger L. Ron Hubbard Series: L. Ron Hubbard's Letters & Journals.

The Early Letters & Journals of
L. Ron Hubbard

A T THE AGE OF SIXTEEN, L. RON HUBBARD TELLS US, HE began to fill the pages of an old account ledger retrieved from his grandfather's attic. It was canvas bound, bore only scant notations from family transactions and otherwise provided ample room to write of "life and dreams and adventure."

Presented in this very special edition of the *L. Ron Hubbard Series* are selections from that journal as well as subsequent journals and letters recounting the same. In the main, these entries span the years 1926 to 1934, or that time of continuous travel between his home in Helena, Montana, the South Pacific where his father served with the United States Navy, the Asia where he witnessed so much that was strange and unusual and Puerto Rico where he conducted his famed mineralogical survey. As a first introductory word, let us say that if nothing sheds more light upon an author's public works than his private papers, the statement is especially pertinent here. For remembering Ron drew heavily from these travels when shaping his later stories, here are the settings for those works. Here is the inscrutable China where a heartbroken officer sails to his death along the Yellow River; here the sullen jungles where tragic leathernecks engage unseen rebels; here, too, those foreboding South Pacific isles where raucous engineers slash roads through impenetrable brush—all the stuff of early tales

Below
USS *Henderson,* aboard which a young Ron Hubbard crossed the Pacific to Asia

Left Puget Sound, Washington, 1927: "Adventure is my guidon"—LRH

soon to catapult him into the forefront of popular literature.

But there is another subject upon which these letters and journals shed much light and that is the young L. Ron Hubbard himself.

Twelve years after filling the last page of his old account ledger, he tells of chancing upon what he wrote and dismissing it as hopelessly adolescent and "most unwise." Yet still later—as a leading figure of American fiction and well along the path of discovery to Dianetics and Scientology—he returned again to that journal and had to concede: "I was right when I was sixteen. I knew things. My opinions were those of today. And so I have advanced in a circle and arrived merely at a better understanding of what ailed me."

What had ailed him, and thus what ultimately drove him on that path of discovery, is also the stuff of these letters and journals: "Our platforms are so frail, our importance so small, our immortality so unassured," he writes from a flyblown Puerto Rican village just shy of his twenty-second birthday. Then outright admitting, "I've discovered a certain presence of philosophy which I'm not supposed to have at my age," he proceeds to pose the proposition of all propositions: "How can we understand that outside us when we can barely realize that which goes on within?" Also scattered through these

Below Ron's boa constrictor belt and spotlessly white pith helmet—absolutely *de rigueur* for Philippine jungles

Left Upon emerging from the Philippine rain forest, 1928

pages are references to the Asian deprivation he would never forget and encounters with those who crashed against "the most horrible things life can offer."

In addition to contemplative letters from the Caribbean and journals from the Chinese mainland, we include his first impressions from Hawaii and Guam, notes from a long night in Haiti, thoughts through restless days in Montana and memories of a perilous trek across the Rocky Mountains. And if, as he elsewhere tells us, these were only the travels of youth and shed little light on what finally came from his greater journey, here, nonetheless, is some of what he recorded on that journey. Here is what he saw, what he felt and what he had to say about it. Then, too, here is a young L. Ron Hubbard who is also the later L. Ron Hubbard. Merely, here he is at the start of his journey when all he knew for certain was: "I feel that I would, in some unclear way, improve the world and that all of my energies are bent toward a reformation for the better and the raising of my fellow man." ∎

A seasoned Asian traveler pauses in San Diego, California, 1929

Off the coast of Guam, 1929;
photograph by L. Ron Hubbard

CHAPTER ONE

A First Word on ADVENTURE

A *First Word on*
Adventure

HAVING TRAVELED A QUARTER OF A MILLION MILES BY the age of nineteen, L. Ron Hubbard knew a thing or two about adventure. Indeed, long before transcontinental flight was even a tangible dream, he had twice crossed the Pacific, weathering typhoons and worse, to explore genuinely exotic lands. As a first word on

such adventures, we open with his 1943 retrospective of life on the road at the dawn of the twentieth century. Written during a brief respite from grueling service through the Second World War, Ron described this journal as "a sketch book more than a diary" and began it with memories of early journeys from his home in Helena, Montana. If his overriding theme seems somewhat wistful, "adventure as I know it, is done," let us bear in mind what would soon follow—namely, the grandest adventure of all into "that vast and hitherto unknown realm half an inch back of our foreheads." But either case, here is the mature LRH glancing back to the young LRH and so providing us an overview of all far-flung travel as he once knew it.

By way of a few ancillary notes, let us understand Ron had been son to a United States naval officer, and if travel was untypical of the day, it was not so for the military family. Hence his allusions to the crossing of limitless deserts (principally the Mojave) en route from the family seat in Helena, Montana, to notoriously drab naval installations along the Southern

Below
Guam, 1927; photograph by L. Ron Hubbard

Left "And I yearned and strained to the sea, always the sea"—LRH along Puget Sound, Washington, 1928

Above
Oakland,
California, 1920:
a nine-year-old
Ron with
grandfather
Lafayette
Waterbury and
Liberty Bill

California coast. Hence, also, his longing for "what I called my HOME. Where I KNEW somebody, where I BELONGED."

As further remarked upon through these pages, however, not all roads were necessarily tedious, not all destinations unwelcoming. For at the age of seven, he explains, "my grandfather took me on an automotive adventure to Portland." To what appears here, let us add: the grandfather in question was

Lafayette Owen Waterbury, a wonderfully adventurous spirit in his own right. The uncle Bob of Tacoma was husband to a Waterbury daughter, late of Portland, Oregon. The trails across the Rockies had been cut by early pioneers, the tires of that Model T Ford tended to blow out every thirty or so miles and Ron occasionally slept in a polar bear rug his father had brought back from a tour with the Great White Fleet. ■

Thursday
14 October 1943

I have just finished reading John Masefield's "Live and Kicking Ned." I am much impressed for I had not known Masefield as the novelist. And I am started by his story upon my own mental adventuring, for he speaks of a strange land within Africa, a nation of whites, the Kranois. If such existed (for they may be but his own creation) they give credence to the theory of "pleasure in adventure."

We are spanning this world a shade too swiftly now for me to dream and will to adventure. I feel a little like a child who tries to see romance in an attic and holds tenaciously as long as he can to his conception, though he well recognizes the substance of object as a disinteresting tangle of old cloth and dust. Adventure, I well know, is in the heart, not in the view. But I find life unbearable under that concept and so refuse to recognize what I know.

The anatomy of adventure has been explored quite often. Young men are born with a will to it, rarely recognize their restlessness with clarity and usually succumb to the softness of Simmons beds and the warmth of a wife. Those who persevere wind up without much worldly reward, the majority inheriting chilblains from the north, malaria from the south and bad digestion from the temperate zone, their sole patrimony besides memory.

I am already in possession of some of this coin—the malaria and the ulcers. I have also multiplied and squared my desire to scratch my feet on far soil. I know that the process of going and the reward of arriving are the one uncomfortable and the other disappointing. It is the horizon one never sees which lures him. And I have come to that state of mind, that supreme disillusion of knowing that nothing waits, that the horizon never seen does not exist. I am restless still. I have no goal short of the planets and stars, for the juke boxes grind in the African veldt and the priests of Thibet smoke Luckies. The A.T.C. flips across the seas and continents in fine disdain of calms and bunions, and today I read with sorrow that a "flying boxcar" carrying three tons of cargo shall now shuttle from coast to coast. That is the beginning of the end of the sea and there will come a day within my lifetime when the lighthouses will go out, one by one and the fast steamers shall go to rot in the muddy corner of the harbor where now the bones of sailing ships thrust forlornly out. I am seeing an era pass. Those around me say, "No, no, that era will not be over ever for heavy cargo will always go by sea." Well, them there newfangled steam vessels weren't no good and wouldn't last, and I dare say that men of the galleys commented amusingly upon the lasting quality of that new idea, sail.

The point is, adventure as I know it, is done. Kipling's great poem, "Romance is Dead" throws a jeer at the engineer, with thousands of steam horses under his hand,

Early Lockheed passenger ship, 1934; photograph by L. Ron Hubbard

who mourns the passing of Romance. But Kipling, whatever his qualities, and I greatly admire them, forgets that Romance and adventure depend in a great measure upon an individual's chances of enhancing his reputation by going far and doing deeds. There must be windmills at which to tilt. There must be fields of courage. And these things must generally be recognized as such by the public at large or they are no fun. Pilots will be so many, so usual, that they will have the social prestige of truck drivers so far as the Romantic and adventurous angle is concerned. I throw no jeer at the engineer who says from his cab, "Romance is Dead." It is dead—or dying.

American forces take with them America. Where they have been, Americans will be again for scores of years. Hollywood will follow. Canned music will follow. The intriguing individualities of the world will be pulled down to a mediocrity. For a thing is not worth seeing unless it has some quality which is its own, which quality should not be so general that it is not novel. Once each state in these United States had its own individuality. In the past twelve years I have seen the last traces vanishing. For the talking picture is a great propaganda medium. It spreads one viewpoint of living and that viewpoint, being a good and decent one, catches hold and kills less strong manifestations. It is growing increasingly difficult to distinguish differences in speech, even between North and South. I can remember how broad they were. But transportation is easy now. People shift readily around. The war has transplanted tens of millions. The population seeks its level of similarity. The individuality of places is vanishing. And so it shall continue to vanish, more rapidly in less of the future, throughout the world. I shall live, perhaps, to see that occur. And what is the use of going to Shanghai when it will so much resemble San Francisco or London or Grand Rapids, Michigan? This is an extreme view, perhaps, but I have seen it.

Returning to the African cities of the Kranois—it would be (and was) exciting to adventure in a world where something as unexpected might be waiting just over the next hill. It is pleasant to think of an era where such things might have been possible. But we are in no such era now. All geographical things are becoming too well known. And as they become well known so shall civilization seek, like water, a common level which shall hold no surprises for such as I.

View of Shanghai, 1927; photograph by L. Ron Hubbard

The Great Era of Adventure is over. The Ocean of the Air has come into its day and outward shall flow Sears Roebuck dresses, Time Magazine and the leaping images of the Lana Turners.

Such a viewpoint is hideous to such as I. There must be wide spaces in which to think, strange music to hear, odd costumes to see and the elements to battle against. Man works toward bringing all things to his heel and killing or leveling all things different from himself. Money, nice cars, good food and a "good job" mean nothing to me when compared to being able to possess the thought that there is a surprise over the horizon.

How does one become this way? Why should one ever permit himself to harbor this odd mania for chilblains, malaria and bad digestion?

In my case I was on my way at the age of three weeks. I had been born in Tilden, Nebraska. As soon as she could travel, my mother took me to her people in Oklahoma. Scarce two, I was taken to Kalispell, Montana, to where my grandfather had removed himself. My father, lately out of the Navy when I was born, got about considerably and I saw little of him that I remember, though I idolized him when he turned up, on rare stops between trips. But when I was three he bought a homestead in Helena, Montana's arid area. When I was seven my grandfather took me on an automotive adventure to Portland, Oregon from Helena, Montana—a Model T Ford, a wilderness almost without trails, rare meetings with other adventurers through the wild Rockies. When I was nine there were other trips with my Father and Mother, trips as far as San Diego, California—and going across the great deserts in a car of those days on the roads of those days *was* an adventure. My Father had entered the Navy again with the declaration of War in 1917. Then, the war over, he was out, a Supercargo on a merchantman to Australia. And then he was in the Navy again. And all this meant movement to me.

At the wheel of the family Buick

When I was very young I was pathetically eager for a HOME. I can remember the trumped up belief (by me) that Helena was my home. I knew a few children there. I had gone a year or two to school there. And I well recall one time, returning there in a car from the Pacific Coast (I was seven) how I wept with eagerness

With father, Harry Ross Hubbard, en route from Helena, Montana, to Oakland, California, 1920

Home at last on the steps of "Old Brick" in Helena, Montana, 1917

at being as near home as Broadwater, a resort near Helena, and how I went hot and cold and laughed and grew hysterical at the realization that I was coming near what I called my HOME. Where I KNEW somebody, where I BELONGED. My grandfather had a big red brick house at the corner of Fifth and Beattie Street, several blocks west of the big state capitol and here were my aunts, my grandparents, my own small possessions. Here was the hub of my Universe. The "Old Brick."

I saw that red brick between the ages of four and seven (living part of that time on the "Old Homestead") and saw it again, briefly, when I was eleven, again briefly when I was sixteen, again when I was eighteen. My Grandfather Waterbury, to whom I was "Buster" died when I was eighteen. The aunts married and were scattered. Recently—four years ago—the "Old Brick" was destroyed in a series of earthquakes.

But the dispersal of people and the final destruction of the house were not what took me out of what was my HOME. My childhood memories consist of being insufferably hot in a swing in an Oklahoma yard (with two goats which butted), of trying desperately to make a little Christmas Tree in Kalispell for my mother who was ill and confined to her room, of watching bluebirds from a tent at the "Old Homestead" (and of the tent blowing down in a screaming storm and my Dad eating cold flapjacks from a bucket in the barn, flapjacks Mother had cooked for him while he thwarted the gale's battle to overturn the stovepipe in the tent), of having lots of fistfights with kids in Helena, of being sickeningly lonely in San Francisco, of Dad carefully abstaining from water when the car broke down in a limitless Nevada desert, of rain at night in Dago, of my uncle Bob's coffee store in Tacoma, of the Olympic Mountains, of the awful abysses below the curling mountain roads of the Rockies, of, in short, many cities, many countrysides. And all this before I was ten.

The Waterbury clan (Ron far left, Grandfather Waterbury, far right) with the Model T Ford of Ron's first automotive adventure

Right The Hubbard family home in Helena, Montana, circa 1925: "Here was the hub of my Universe. The 'Old Brick.'"—LRH

"Dad carefully abstaining from water when the car broke down in a limitless Nevada desert"—LRH

At another transitory residence for a short-lived stay in Seattle, Washington, 1923

I had seen most of the United States when I was fourteen. But sometimes I had gone HOME.

Each time I went home I expected, of course, to find things as I had left them. They never were for scenes and people change and unless one continues himself in the same environment his own change is not *their* change. So each time I came HOME I was different, HOME was different and as though making a V in time, HOME and I diverged, wider and wider.

When sixteen, I crossed the Pacific. And again. And then I crossed it twice more and I was not yet eighteen. I saw the Orient, went through it twice. Mexico and Canada I had seen when I was twelve—and Panama too. When I was twenty-one I had seen the Indies, the West Indies, and knew them well. I had lived all over.

My Mother must feel guilty about my moving around so much for she always misunderstands me when I mention my lack of a Home. True enough she made a home wherever we went and did it well for she is a clever woman. But one cannot move around without losing his intimacy with his surroundings, that intimacy being born only from long association. School after school. Dozens of schools. I began to hate school. As a redhead I had little chance of being branded as other than a rebel.

How sick I became of riding in cars. How ghastly to me appeared trains. But I loved the sea. I loved steamers and sailboats and surf and sailors. And I yearned and strained to the sea, always the sea, for it is a lovely, vicious lonely thing. In its limitless variety I had a sort

Panama Canal, 1923

of HOME. There were surprises waiting on the other shore. And I saw the sea with an imaginative eye and peopled it today with all its dead yesterday. I was very, very young when I knew its tropical sunrises, its northern fog.

Oh, the anguish, the depression, the tragedy of youth! When I was sixteen I began to write in a big account ledger I had pirated from the "Old Brick." I had lots to write about and in Puget Sound, at sea, in Washington, D.C., in Helena, in Guam, I scribbled away. I wrote in a vein of outraged despair, wrote of Life and dreams and emotions and adventure. Then when I was twenty-two I found them and considered them childish, adolescent, most unwise. Then when I was twenty-eight I knew how childish and adolescent I was at twenty-two. And now at thirty-two I have seen again what I wrote when I was sixteen. I was right when I was sixteen. I knew things. My opinions were those of today. And so I have advanced in a circle and arrived merely at a better understanding of what ailed me when I was in my teens, and know that it still ails me.

I have all the world around me. My walls are 180 East Longitude and 90 North and 90 South Latitude. And no man can stand such a large room. Man's mind is constructed to be bounded by the lines of a town or a county or a small sea so that he can think quietly and wonderfully on what may lie beyond it and yet feel secure of what lies within it. For my plight, you see, is knowing what is over the horizon. And having no place this side of it.

Adventure is my guidon. And now with the Ocean of the Air taking away all the surprises which might remain and with Mankind too puny, too cowardly, to conquest the outer space, I am here, here with the Will to Go, with nowhere to go. Here with no plumed hat, no rapier, no cloak. Here with no fair ship of my own and no fair destination if I had one. Here with the clang and whine and greasy grab of commerce all around me, here with the blind eyes and still tongues of the Juke Box Generation all about me, here with a sick heart, knowing that I get no younger, here but all alone.

But have you ever been on a frontier? Have you ever felt valued for yourself just because you are a lonely man in a lonely land and met with one

"When I was sixteen I began to write in a big account ledger I had pirated from the 'Old Brick'"—LRH

With hikers in Washington State's Cascade Mountain range, 1923. Ron, front row, far right.

such as you? Have you ever felt the clannishness of frontiersmen, the warm faith in the might of the friend beside you? For the world out there, when it was lonely, when it was new, demanded certain things of the individual or else he lived not long and amongst the things demanded were a certain courage and a certain camaraderie. Men had to be big or fall before the unknown. And man had to have friends.

Back in the teens of this damnable 20th Century did you ever go for a trip in your brand-new broken-down Maxwell? If you did, you can recall the feeling that you were really undertaking something. Your voyage was beset by flat tires and perchance by stalling engine. And when you drove along that lonely road, a rare being in a rare vehicle, you found another car, you were exceedingly pleased. You perhaps saw the fellow was in trouble and you stopped. Or he wasn't in trouble and you both stopped. You passed the time of day. You remarked in unkind phrases on the ruts in this dusty road, you felt quite pleased to see him, quite happily drawn to a fellow adventurer. You two were beating the road, the flat tires, the bad gasoline. And you were comrades. And it was rare that you didn't take time to stop and it was rare that you didn't get help when you needed it.

Get a flat tire on a four-pass highway today and see how many stop. And realize that the world has become a four-pass highway.

The Great Wall of China, 1928;
photograph by L. Ron Hubbard

CHAPTER TWO

ASIAN DIARIES

A fishing craft putting
out to sea
WANG PO RIVER
CHINA

Asian Diaries

ALTHOUGH WHEN GENERALLY SPEAKING OF LRH adventures in Asia, one is typically referencing his travels across northern China circa 1928, his first taste of the Orient actually came a year earlier with his father's posting at the United States Navy's refueling station on the island of Guam. In consequence, the sixteen-year-old Ron and his mother embarked upon a roundabout voyage to that "Asiatic Station." Also in consequence, and compiled from handwritten notes en route, comes Ron's typewritten journal of sketches from ports of call at Hawaii, Japan, Hong Kong and Shanghai.

If the Asia of his journal seems grim and dispirited, the view is fully accurate. Having leapt from stagnant feudalism to a furious capitalism in the space of two generations, Japan was indeed no longer "the happy land pictured so in stories." Better than half the indigenous labor force earned less than 48 cents a day, the great slums of Osaka could not even be ignored in the tourist guides, while the paupers Ron references in Kobe numbered more than twenty thousand. Likewise, China was no happy land in that summer of 1927. To put it very bluntly—and this from LRH friend and author Will Durant—"the most powerful feeling in China today is hatred of foreigners."

Hawaii, however, had still been a reasonably unspoiled paradise and following from Ron's description of surfboard riding at Waikiki, he would actually number among the first to surf Southern California waves. ■

```
                PROPERTY
                   OF
            RONALD HUBBARD
            736 - Fifth Avenue
              Helena, Montana
```

June thirtieth came at last and we were eager to trade the humdrum life of Frisco for the quiet restfulness of thirty-four days at sea. When the President Madison pulled away from the pier, I felt a catch in my throat at leaving the United States for even a short space of time. The Ferry Building gradually receded and then the Golden Gate was gone from view. Miles of tumultuous water surrounded us and the great engines of the ship throbbed on into the west.

Even the deck stewards looked rather bleary next morning and a crowd of pale faces decorated deck chairs and the rail. Seasick? "Certainly not. How silly! Only something we ate!"

Mother felt fit as a fiddle and was tactless enough to show herself above. Thus making herself unpopular with the menu-broadcasters for the rest of the voyage.

I had fun playing a game called shuffleboard and another called deck golf. Some of the men kept talking of salt pork and slippery oysters, but I kept my colors flying through pitch and roll.

Six days later at dawn we hurried on deck to view Hawaii. Coming into the harbor at Honolulu, all the beach boys swam out to the ship to dive for quarters. It used to be pennies. Thus has the Hawaiian developed his commerce.

A Hawaiian princess aboard was received by the Royal Hawaiian Band, and a quartet of women greeted her with native songs. Friends greeted friends with leis of flowers.

Friends of ours showed us the town and country. The Pali is beautiful and historic. Two thousand warriors jumped to their death from this cliff rather than surrender to the king.

Hawaii is quiet, peaceful and interesting. Nobody hurries. There may be a law against it.

I swam at famous Waikiki and rode a surfboard. The waves here are much longer than those in

Along Tumon Beach, Guam, 1927

Left President Madison at dock in Hong Kong, 1927; photograph by L. Ron Hubbard

Mt. "FUJI" from Panorama near Lake Shoji.
望展士冨りよマラノパ湖進精

"Fujiyama came into view fifty miles at sea.... It has a celestial beauty that distinguishes it from all other mountains."—LRH

California and sometimes attain the speed of sixty miles an hour.

Leaving Honolulu filled us with regret and we stayed on deck for two hours watching the city and Diamond Head fade into the distance.

Westward tugged the ship's twelve thousand horses. Two days out of Honolulu summer clothes were replaced by winter overcoats.

The second engineer took me in hand and showed me over the ship, a complete city afloat; the galley, spotless with shining equipment and Chinese cooks who grinned and displayed blank teeth; the great engines; the fireroom, so hot the plates were red and the oil fire white; the metal "Mike" which guides the ship by radio.

Still hale and hearty we began to anticipate Yokohama, the city of the earthquake. Fujiyama came into view fifty miles at sea, first seen above the clouds. A symmetrical cone, it has a celestial beauty that distinguishes it from all other mountains. The pink robe of snow suggests a garment for royalty.

Early in the morning we began to wind our way among the reefs that menace the harbor entrance to Yokohama. Japanese subs, seaplanes and destroyers gave us the lookover.

Guarding the harbor entrance at one time were two forts, for at the time of the quake Japan was all set for a nice, little war with someone. The South fort was hideously scrambled and seventeen hundred men within its walls were crushed. So shaken were the foundations that it cannot be rebuilt and the bodies of the soldiers could not be recovered. The other fort lost a thousand men in its falling walls, but it has been rebuilt.

Having passed quarantine, our ship went in alongside the dock. Only the huge concrete base was left after the quake and the warehouses were not rebuilt on the dock. After seeing Yokohama one can realize what a horror an earthquake can be.

On the seaward side of our ship the unloading took place in great lighters. Aboard those lighters families make their homes and the women work beside their men with babies strapped on papoose fashion.

Ashore we saw sights that make the slums of our own cities almost tolerable. So few of the poor were clean and many covered with sores. The rickshaw boys' clothing had a permanent cocoon look, but the rickshaws were clean with white laundered covers.

At nine o'clock the next night we reached Kobe. All the passengers went ashore, some to shop, others to go to eat Sukiyaki and drink Saki. (Incidentally we got stuck in a shopping party and it was not until after we were in Guam some time that we had our Sukiyaki dinner, cooked especially for us by the Japanese restaurant proprietor.)

Kobe's Main Street is a brilliantly lighted, highly pirated shopping district for the especial attraction of tourists. To purchase real Japanese articles necessitates visiting the dark narrow by-streets, and small upstairs shops where prices are surprisingly low.

The shoes worn by these people are heavy things made of wood, held on by clenching the toes. They are left on the outer step of the house or shop, so that the acquiring of a pair of new shoes is simplified.

The clothes of the men consist of a European felt hat, a gray cloak tied with a big sash containing pockets and a pair of shoes about four inches high. The women wear trousers, ankle length, a high-necked, loose-sleeved coat and slippers. Their hair is combed straight back and held with hairpins. The geisha girls wear the fancy headdress and the big bow decorated kimono and shoes five inches high.

Going back to the ship in our rickshaws about one in the morning, we saw many beggars bedded down for the night in the dirty streets. They lay down to sleep anywhere any time sleep overcomes them. They were a diseased looking lot.

Next morning we were steaming through the famous Inland Sea. Queer little boats were around us. The land each side rose in mountain terraces intensively cultivated. Water and sky were a deep blue. About four in the afternoon we passed two cities on opposite shores, about two miles apart. Ferries were plying back and forth, huge chimneys on factories smoking and evidence of great activity. Picturesque at a distance, the close-up was probably the usual congestion of population and the dirt.

The most impressive sight in all the ports was the great amount of shipping, all the commercial

A Grand Kabuki theatrical performance as depicted on a postcard purchased in Kobe, 1927 countries of the world were represented. Fishing is a great industry and in the Inland Sea there were thousands of fishing boats. Some of them were queer ones, with eyes carved in front and a little man with a big hat and a short coat worked the unwieldy oar that served as rudder. These boats carry the entire family. Cooking is done on a charcoal stove, the invariable meal boiled fish and boiled rice. Flour is unknown and other vegetables are too expensive.

The whole channel is dotted with hamlets. In spite of the green, terraced hills, there is a dreary look to it all. It doesn't look the happy land pictured so in stories.

We knew when we reached the Yellow Sea for it is aptly named. We reached the Yangtze at nine in the evening and lay outside all night. At daybreak we sailed into the dirty but swift current. There is an enormous delta fast pushing out to sea. The mouth of the river is so wide and the shores so far away there is little to see. Where the river divides, entering the Wang Po, the real river sights begin with ships of every description and nation.

The first flag to greet us was the Stars and Stripes floating over the stern of a destroyer. Millions of fishing boats and junks caught our attention. Some of them were tied up to the wharves and had not been away from their moorings for three hundred years. They had eyes carved on their bows and a shark's tail on the forward mast. Some of the people on these river boats had never been ashore.

At the Dollar docks two miles above Shanghai we anchored. No customs to bother here and we went ashore at nine o'clock in the morning. Such a ragged, discrepant lot of Chinese were around the waterfront. They live worse than anyone in the world and earn about fifteen cents a day when a job can be had. (Fifteen cents Mex at that.) They can live on ten centavos a day, rather exist.

Such a racket unloading ship. Two coolies can balance five hundred pounds on a bamboo pole and trot off singing. One cries "Yahee" and the other in turn "Yoho," a

tone or so lower. Just those two notes over and over. It is weird as a death chant. It goes on from dawn to dark, all to earn fifteen cents Mex.

The puffy little "Billy Dollar" snorted up to the landing and took us over across the river to Shanghai, the "Paris of the Orient." The two miles down the river and across takes nearly an hour. A crumby Portuguese man-o'-war swung at her cable. Alongside was an American destroyer very smart and snappy. Farther down were

Chinese coinage, colloquially known as "Mex"

the Pittsburgh and more destroyers and the transport Henderson. French, English, Japanese and Italian war vessels added to the formidable appearance.

Little fishing boats have an annoying way of rushing across the bows of the big liners. They do this to cut off the river devils, and often they barely miss being cut in two.

We took a French car through the Bund to the Palace Hotel in Shanghai. Mr. Moran of Seattle, chief officer of the Madison, borrowed a car from a friend in Shanghai and his chauffeur took us through the British and French Concessions, up Bubbling Well Road and across to a small part of the native city outside the barbed wire entanglements. Sikh policemen were everywhere. They are big dark bearded fellows and in their turbans and short trousers of khaki look picturesque. They carry great rattan sticks and a rifle slung across the back. Tommy Atkins was very much in evidence and the American marines, as well as Japanese and British marines.

Rickshaws were thick as sin. The drivers run or rather take a swinging pace. The Japanese rickshaw man does a bouncing trot.

Shanghai Harbor, China, 1927; photograph by L. Ron Hubbard

Coolies, rickshaws and
THE INEVITABLE MARINE

Opening down the main avenue over which our car traveled were hundreds of narrow intriguing streets, teeming with life. Great fish floated here and there and paper banners hung overhead. The stores were stocked with every sort of junk. Dried fish rattled on strings in the wind. Queer looking foods and dry goods were side by side.

On the outside of the British Concession I saw a British Tommy take a Chinaman by the coat and knock him across the street. The unpoliced part of the native city is forbidden ground. On the Bubbling Well Road is the girl market, but this place is now used to quarter British soldiers.

On this road is a beautiful hotel once the home of a Chinese gentleman. The grounds are laid out with pergolas and fountains and the hotel has tapestries and mosaic tile floors.

Junks in Shanghai Harbor, 1927;
photograph by L. Ron Hubbard

The French Concession is untidy and the buildings are all behind high walls.

We joined the Madison crowd for the tiffin at the Palace Hotel and afterwards visited some of the shops. We saw flawless jade and wonderful tapestries and rugs. Only the junk was cheap and that was not worth carrying home.

Hong Kong came next. It is a city very British on the surface and very native underneath. Just off Queen Street the district is all native and very dirty. Beggars sleep on the sidewalk at night and all day cry for "cumshaw."

Hong Kong has an extremely low humidity and is very depressingly hot. We returned to the Hong Kong Hotel for refreshments as usual. A jolly lime squeeze suited our thirst. By that time I had purchased an elephant hat and was tempted to wear shorts and be as comfortable as Tommy.

Hong Kong is built on an island and the Dollar docks are on the mainland. The money is all Mex (worth one half U.S. gold). The ferry trip from Kowloon across to Hong Kong costs a nickel.

On the Kowloon side the walk to the Madison led through the inevitable mass of working coolies, very dirty and not caring where they spit. The heat was insufferable by afternoon and aided by our first tropical rain we were not sorry to leave.

Sikh policeman, Shanghai;
photograph by L. Ron Hubbard

Left "Coolies, rickshaws and THE INEVITABLE MARINE";
photograph and caption by L. Ron Hubbard

Two days later we arrived in Manila with very little ado. Manila Bay is a big body of water, very dirty. The tide was so bad we could scarcely dock. We had a struggle trying to unload our luggage.

Away from Hong Kong we rather regretted that our trip was so near an end. The dancing, the excellent cuisine and all of the pomp were things not easily discarded. However, I was anxious to "lamp" the "Gold Star" which was to take us to Guam.

Every ship we'd pass, some frivolous passenger would sing out "there's the Blue Star." They had the naval ladies worried sick telling them about the horrors of the Typhoon belt from Manila to Guam.

We weighed anchor the next afternoon aboard the "Gold Star" upon the last hop of our momentous journey to Guam. Then ensued seven days of rough weather and rotten grub.

Even my Uke and Sax failed to cheer me.

Late in the evening we sighted the isle of Guam. It was not much, in fact, just a low line on the dusky horizon. The navigator took his bearings, and we stood on and off all night.

When morning came we steamed cautiously up to the harbor and then in through the reef-bound mouth. A 6-80 came out to meet us and apparently no customs or medical inspection need be. Dad was on the next small craft, and we were sure glad to see him. *Ron*

Left Agana, Guam, 1927; photograph by L. Ron Hubbard

Right Guam, 1927: "The island is rather unsettled"—LRH

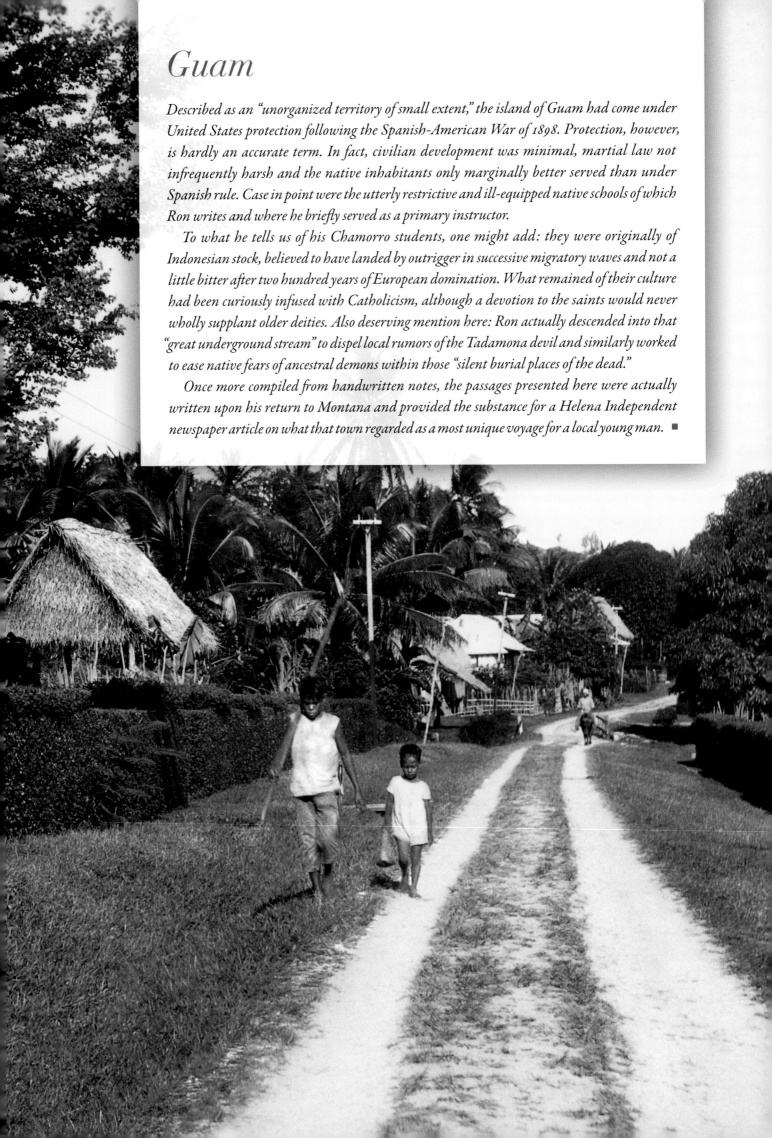

Guam

Described as an "unorganized territory of small extent," the island of Guam had come under United States protection following the Spanish-American War of 1898. Protection, however, is hardly an accurate term. In fact, civilian development was minimal, martial law not infrequently harsh and the native inhabitants only marginally better served than under Spanish rule. Case in point were the utterly restrictive and ill-equipped native schools of which Ron writes and where he briefly served as a primary instructor.

To what he tells us of his Chamorro students, one might add: they were originally of Indonesian stock, believed to have landed by outrigger in successive migratory waves and not a little bitter after two hundred years of European domination. What remained of their culture had been curiously infused with Catholicism, although a devotion to the saints would never wholly supplant older deities. Also deserving mention here: Ron actually descended into that "great underground stream" to dispel local rumors of the Tadamona devil and similarly worked to ease native fears of ancestral demons within those "silent burial places of the dead."

Once more compiled from handwritten notes, the passages presented here were actually written upon his return to Montana and provided the substance for a Helena Independent newspaper article on what that town regarded as a most unique voyage for a local young man. ∎

The island is rather unsettled inland. The Spanish had it long enough to make several interesting touches in the customs and to leave many antiques of great value. Outside of this they have nothing to show but a depleted population, and the establishment of the Catholic Church.

It is said that at one time, the language and people were very civilized. At that time there were supposed to be one hundred thousand inhabitants. These people were killed off during the great small-pox epidemic, late in the nineteenth century. There are only 15,000 natives at present.

The superstitions are intensely interesting. The "great cheese ghost" is named "Tadamona." He is supposed to dwell on "Missionary Point" and to ramble around after midnight. He has a man shape at times and attains the height of the cocoanut trees. Again he is seen in the form of a beautiful woman. The former brings sickness and disease, and the latter good luck. Should you ask a native whether or not he has seen either of them, instead of saying "yes" he explains them and makes ambiguous remarks about him.

It is a known fact that the island at one time was a kingdom because of the "latis" sacrificial stones, and graves that have their feet to the sea. They were also cannibals at one time as the remains of several feasts are reputed to be in evidence.

Our houseboy, Jesus, was typical Chamorro. It sure was tough on him to see me depart. He was shock-headed and his skin was nearly as dark as his hair. It seems queer to me that they take the name Jesus for so many of their children. I do not think that there are over a dozen names on the whole island. The one next in abundance is "Inaquin" which is followed by "Francisco" and "Francisca."

Their eyes are for the most part brown, though blue eyes are not infrequent. Against such a dark skin the latter shows up beautifully. To my notion, their whole appearance is ruined by their teeth. They indulge in the "betel nut" habit as do the people of the Philippines

Right Ron's Chamorro friend, Jesus, 1927;
photograph and hand tinting by L. Ron Hubbard

Left "The Paradise that never was," Guam, 1927;
photograph by L. Ron Hubbard

"It is a known fact that the island at one time was a kingdom because of the 'latis' sacrificial stones, and graves that have their feet to the sea"—LRH; photograph by L. Ron Hubbard

and India. This small nut is not harmful to the constitution, but it makes the lips a fiery red and the teeth a coal black. It gives you the impression that they have pyorrhea, but it cannot be so because more than four out of five have it. The women do not need rouge because of it.

The old forts there rear their turrets at various places on the island. An especially interesting one is the fort of San Luis d'Apra in Apra Harbor. Its doors have been sealed for years and, as if to hide the structure, vines wind themselves about it. The walls were built with remarkable skill, especially the corners. Most of the prison and the turret have been eroded and have fallen into decay, but the powder house and firing steps remain. The walks that once heard the rhythm of a sentry's beat, and the crash of the evening gun are now the running place of lizards. One cannot imagine the solitude and depression that surrounds it. All that beauty and grandeur which surrounded it yesterday has faded as the rose which dies and leaves its thorn.

The rolling hills inland are covered with thick vegetation, which is a deep green in a contrast to the sky and sea. Though it is not hard to penetrate, a thousand mysteries seem to surround it. The silent burial places of the dead who lived long ago are likely to come as a shock to one who has thoughts of lovelier things.

A great underground stream is the source of a great deal of wonder. Below the earth several hundred feet, the bats flit on mysterious errands and the spider weaves his never varying pattern. Light filters in at long intervals as the water swishes gently beneath. A similar formation is said to have occurred at "Missionary Point" the purported abode of the devil "Tadamona." The only difference is the salt water in lieu of the fresh. Queer noises result from the action of the waves, so no wonder it is the home of a "haunt."

The old fetes or fiestas are still quite the thing. The native drink, "aguardiente" aids the former. These parties are given for weddings, deaths, or some church holiday. One evening Teddy, Harold and I took the notion into our heads that we would like to see what the natives of San Antonio, the tough end of town, were doing. On the outskirts we heard snatches of foolish songs and the blat of ancient and discrepant instruments. Teddy went ahead to reconnoiter and

"A Spanish fort. Shows the well built corner."—LRH; photograph by L. Ron Hubbard

we followed. Finally we reached the shacks from which the supposed music was issuing. All about it stood natives that were rapidly losing their sense of balance. Something whizzed out of the window and over my head to light with a crash. A "dead soldier." A man came out of the low door and passed a box, containing the betel nut, among his guests. Then a guitar struck up a plaintive Spanish melody. It was readily joined by the accordion and saxophone, which had been responsible for the hideous racket that had first met our ears.

We soon found ourselves within the hot, frail structure of the nipa bahai. People in various stages of drunkenness were all about us. In the center of the tiny room stood the would-be music makers, while all about them reeled the dancers. In the corner sat the bride with her father on her left and her husband at her right. A man reeled up to us with a handful of the inevitable betel nut. He did not like my looks so he started something and we lit out for home.

"Byway of Agana"—LRH; photograph by L. Ron Hubbard

The religious faith of the Chamorro was regulated by the Spanish, who are Catholics. Catholicism has furnished them many superstitions as it has in the Philippines. Doctors who have studied them believe that "Tadamona" was invented to force the payment of church dues.

Before I left the States, several naval officers kidded me about red hair. They told me that everyone with red hair was made a king upon reaching Guam. Of course I thought that it was mere buffoonery and I laughed it off. When I got to Guam, all the natives would stare at me in wonder. Whenever I sat down outside of a doorway, the children would gather around with a very dumb and astonished look upon their faces. The real test came when I commenced a teacher's career. The Chamorroettes would not study, they would just look at my hair. My gaudy locks were better than any written passport known. I walked about the streets after dark and all of the natives I passed would suddenly shut up. I sometimes wonder what I ever did to deserve red hair.

The natives play a queer instrument called a "Billibutugun." It is about seven feet long and has a piece of baling wire strung across it. They hold the wire taut by the spring of the stick and place the cocoanut, which is nailed to the center of the stick on their stomachs. It is said that the larger the stomach,

Chamorro with the native musical instrument, "Billibutugun," circa 1927; photograph by L. Ron Hubbard

the better the tone. Maybe so. I heard a fellow play "Ain't gonna rain no more" on the thing. Very "tin-panny," but quite recognizable.

Our houseboy, "Jaquin" claimed that he had seen the great ghost, "Tadamona," so I told him that I'd go down to Missionary (or Siesta) Point about midnight some night just to see if I could see him. I was half kidding and half in earnest. Should one live amongst people for a couple of months with little more to do than study the people, they might understand just how the firmest of scorn may be shaken.

The martial naval law of Guam is very strict and un-compromising. The Governor has the full power to make or break any law he chooses. The marines are always in serious fights that start over petty things. It is the tropics I guess.

Our house is of great dimensions. It is very nicely laid out. It was not fully decorated until about three or four days before I left. Then it was beautiful. Parasites from banana trees grew on the wall and the green and buff of the furniture and walls matched them perfectly. Under soft yellow lights, the shiny black floors of ifil wood reflected everything. The windows are free from glass and are covered with screens.

The outer harbor is usually filled with sharks and other carnivores. I have watched them from the deck of the "Gold Star." One great fish swam lazily to and fro waiting for the garbage to be thrown out. His great fin protruded from the water now and then while he looked at the ship. With the aid of a pair of glasses, I saw his little yellow and black eyes roll at times. He even blinked. Sharks are the one fish that have lids over their eyes. I have recently read that sharks will not attack a human being. I think this to be decidedly untrue. Although a Hawaiian may dive among them unharmed, I have heard of white men losing legs and arms and at times even killed outright. It is exceedingly queer that men make such queer statements just to appear "sage." _Ron_

Left Chamorro children "strike a pose" on a wash day, Agat, Guam, 1927; photograph by L. Ron Hubbard

Right Tumon, Guam: way station to Asia

Homeward-bound aboard the Nitro

Licensed to captain vessels of any size on any ocean, the name L. Ron Hubbard has a long and distinguished association with things nautical. To cite but a few points of interest, there was his service at the helm of hard-pressed expeditionary vessels, his command of warships through the Second World War and his training of famously competent crews. In a very real sense, however, it all began when a sixteen-year-old LRH stepped aboard a Seattle-bound USS Nitro for a first taste of service at sea. In contrast to the outgoing Madison, the Nitro was a no-frills, battle-ready troop transport regularly plying between Asiatic Stations and the Pacific Northwest and Ron had only received passage as the able-bodied son of a naval officer. In addition to what is cited here, he would elsewhere speak of apprenticing at the navigator's desk and actually helping to work those new oil turbines. Not mentioned, but also of interest: the pages of this day-by-day account were typed on a borrowed Remington or Underwood and, as even the keystrokes suggest, composed through some fairly heavy seas. ∎

Saturday 16, 1927. Aboard the USS Nitro.

Got up at six. Shot a roll on the way to Piti. Went aboard at 6:45 A.M. Breakfasted aboard.

8:00—Mother and Dad went ashore on Film boat. Weighed anchor and left Guam. Dropped Pilot Docker. Waves high on reef.

12:00—Luggage arranged to liking. My room-mates are Dick Derickson and Jerry Curtis. Nice chaps. Dick is from Seattle too. He was at Camp Parsons the same time that I was. In 1925.

4:00—Had a good sleep. Looked the bridge over. Dinner. Saw "Three Faces East." Viewed a beautiful moon come up, and felt rather lonely. The cloud effect was gorgeous. The moon looked like an illuminated globe and then it dived under a cloud to begin its task of riding the sky. Bed, sweet bed. My foot looks better but it is still painful. Doctor said it would still be exposed to infection. It had better heal before I get to Hawaii.

Sunday 17, 1927. Aboard USS Nitro.

Got up though it is Sunday. That is not even regarded on this man's ship. 9:00—Straightened up room and visited sick bay. Lt. Com. Welden, the exec, told us to appoint someone to take charge of the quarters. We appointed Jerry or rather sentenced him. I'm on tomorrow. These Filipino hombres sure are nasty, but they won't stay that way long. Our floor is sadly in need of a mopping. I'll see to it tomorrow. Chow is good and the officers are nice though I see little of them. My foot is better. The Medic probed it again.

Our room is o.k. I slept below but tonight I'm going above. I take two baths a day so it takes a deal of bandage and alcohol. —Hard to keep the old place straight. Plenty of drawer space. Haven't read much. I'm going to study history tomorrow. —There is a soda fountain aboard though I don't inhabit the place. These sailors sure are "Acey Deucey" fiends all day long.

July 18, 1927.

Almost got rained on last night. Good sleep too. Broke out Blaz's fruit from the chill room. —The bananas are green but they'll ripen. The alligator pears are ripe, and very good. We brought up a small bunch of bananas, a cocoanut and a pear. Jerry is still in bed and it is ten. Dick and I were up at six. Sure miss Guam. Good show tonight. —My foot feels fine.

Left The USS *Nitro,* Puget Sound, Washington, circa 1925

July 19, 1927.

At six this morning we came below so the gobs could wash down the deck and as I had a headache I turned in down below. Dick was the "middie" for the day. (We have the title now.) And he did not wake Jerry or me for chow so we slept until eleven. Now, every day, we have had the room ready for inspection and not a soul has looked us over, but today at ten it seems the captain came poking around and found the room in terrible shape so he reported us to the exec who sent for Dick (who had been up since six). Then Dick came back and routed us out as the exec had ordered us to appear before him as soon as possible. He sure seemed mad. Jerry and I were respectful but he sure bawled us out. Then we came back and fixed the room to the guards. Sure did shine but he wouldn't even look at it. —My foot feels great. I can walk without limping, but it is still sore on top. —Played my sax but got no complaint. It is working nicely. (The sax.) The place sure looks nice now. —It turned a little chilly but not cool enough for blues. I've been up on the bridge several times. Jerry has atrocious manners and the Warrants don't like him. He's sloppy and so is his dunnage. —Awful movie tonight. Both Dick and Jerry are homesick etc., but they can be cheered up, which is something as neither is far from weeping. The Warrants have been kidding us that we stop at Wake Island so we'd better write. Ha. —To bed because of what the exec told us. I'm sleeping under a 5-inch gun tonight.

July 20, 1927.

Aboard Nitro at Sea. Calm, cirrus clouds on horizon. 2,276 to go last night at 8:00 Chaumont 602 miles astern P.S.C. 77 one hour advanced. —Sighted Wake Island about 10:30. Went fishing with exec. Many fish. That is the only reason we stopped. Very rough. We almost dove a few times. The punt that the whaleboat towed had trouble staying away from the ship's exhaust. Exec caught 8 fish, four of which got away. —The place is very low on the horizon, the highest point being 21 feet. The beach is very deceiving. It looks very gradual but is actually perpendicular. It is almost a horseshoe in shape as a big lagoon rests in the dip. Many strange and beautiful birds are in evidence. They are so tame that they will not move though they are sitting on their eggs. All the nests are on the ground as the highest shrub is 8 feet. There are about 8 square miles in the place. The fish look at you fearlessly and should you throw a rock at them, they would flock around it to see what it was. Mr. Borne caught a bird and had his picture taken with it, then he let it go. A Marine Lieut. named Edgar Allen Poe is aboard collecting material for a book. He went swimming in the lagoon. The Nitro stood on and off about a mile out waiting for us all the while as it was too deep to anchor. The water there is so intensely blue that a jug of it is slightly tinted. The bottom was 30 fathoms down and it looked as though it were four feet. Very beautiful and covered with sea life; coral, (dead and living) and fish. Sharks and Barracuda are all around. —There are two houses for the shipwrecked and two water tanks which are filled by the geodetic survey every three months. The fish in the lagoon are plentiful and multi-colored. They looked like a Fourth of July parade. Lucky no ladies were around today. The exec sure can swear. —About twenty went ashore and most of the officers fished while the men towed them around. Sure is a desolate place. Nothing, not even a palm breaks the sky. Beautiful weird clouds are always upon the horizon and not a sail breaks its line. All day long the birds wheel but they rarely scream, as if they were afraid of breaking the gripping silence. A shipwrecked mariner would not be worth saving after two weeks of this. —Under weigh at 2:00.

July 21, 1927.

Nothing doing today except a fight over the Dempsey-Sharkey bout. Very dead and nearly everyone has lost the old gift of gab pro-tem.

July 22, 1927.

Today is Friday. This morning I got up early to study. Tomorrow will also be today.

July 22, 1927.

Bright cracks are floating around such as "What was I doing at this time today?" It seems queer to be seven days out of Guam but not to have had a week pass. We pass 180 degrees at 12:00 midnight, the INT.D.T.L. —A good many of the crew are out their pay for months to come because of this fight. —There is a fountain aboard and yesterday I saw a monster of a man, old navy style with all the brawn, licking an ice cream cone. Ha. Thus is the navy. The efficiency aboard is great, another ha.

July 23, 1927.

While I was on the bridge with Mr. McCrory today he sighted what turned out to be a spar. He thought it was a derelict and was all ready to throttle the engines. I went down into the engine room today where I received a very cordial welcome. These engines can turn out 20,000 H.P. and then some. The revs. of the prop. are 105 p/m. on the average making a speed of 13.5 to 14.7. The engines themselves are the new oil turbines. The two huge condensers are larger than the engines, strange as it may seem. The ice plant is a marvel but I don't like the white, porous ice it turns out. It is clean and cold though so I should kick? The propeller shafts are larger than the Madison's. If this ship is the cream of the naval duty, I'll sure stick to milk. The officers work about an hour and then sit around and look bored. The enlisted personnel bear the brunt of the work. I guess responsibility offsets it though.

July 24, 1927.

Here it is Sunday. No church though, and though I rarely go, the fact I couldn't made me want to. I read the New Testament clear through. Mr. Mason (he's about 22nd ensign) had me on the bridge at eight telling me all about the constellations. Never in my life have I seen such beauties. The sky is alive with them. The "Milky Way" looks like a white cloud. Tonight says goodbye to the moon. I wish it had waited until we get to Honolulu. I've never seen anything like it. The "Southern Cross" was wonderful, but not like I thought it would be. I think that the "Swan" is more like a cross. One gets sentimental over the stars without the moon anywhere.

View from the *Nitro*'s crow's nest, 1927; photograph by L. Ron Hubbard

July 25, 1927.

Today I was the first to sight port of the Hawaiian Islands. Lt. Brown said I might climb up to the lookout in the crow's nest. He also told me to wake the lookout up, as there was land off the port bow. I said "Aye Aye" and got off the bridge. A moment later found me staring up the forward mast which looked ungodly high. I overcame a nervous tremor and climbed a rope up to the steel ladder rather than get around the greasy stuff surrounding the mast. Nice prospect a fall was. Then I

"I tackled the first fifty feet of ladder. It surely looked and felt unsubstantial."—LRH; photograph by L. Ron Hubbard

tackled the first fifty feet of ladder. It surely looked and felt unsubstantial. About halfway up I thought I'd never been so nervous before. After that ladder came an even smaller steel ladder. Up I went, all confidence by this time. In a moment I reached the nest and sure enough there was the lookout reading a "Western Story." He invited me to climb in. The last in itself is worse than the rest of it all put together. One has to dangle with nothing under him and work halfway around to the other edge. Over the side of the box I swung and then in. My God what a relief! The deck was doing all sorts of crazy things, as some sea was running. There had been quite a bit of breeze for days, but today it was awful. Going up it nearly blew me off twice. —Sure enough there was the land. I sighted it as 2 points off the port bow through to the bridge. Then I skiddled down. Scared? I hope to sneer. Then after I got down I really was *weak*.

July 26, 1927.

Saw the city of Honolulu this morning as we went into Pearl Harbor Navy Yard. Very nice to see the place again. We could not go ashore until the customs came aboard and they never came so we

Nuuanu Pali, Honolulu, Hawaii: "Nobody hurries. There may be a law against it."—LRH

went at one P.M. A little later I found myself landing at the sub-base and walking to the train station. After a fifteen minute ride on the puffy little train we were in Honolulu. I went out to the Moana with Dick and Jerry. We went our ways.

July 27, 28, 29th.

Today all were back aboard ship by nine A.M. as we sailed at ten. I did not take many pictures in Hawaii as I found there are few to be taken. Compared to Guam the place is not tropical enough to be pretty or Northern enough to have beautiful scenery; hence I returned to the ship with the Kodak still empty. I did a lot of swimming and the Hass' took me around quite a little. I got to see the "Pali." It surely is awe-inspiring. A thousand feet straight down and such a wind! Glad we are under weigh again. Paid my mess bill, it came to more than I thought it would. However the chow is swell.

July 30, 1927.

I'm recuperating from my shore leave today. Hope I can recover.

July 31, 1927.

About ten I put some tennis shoes on and went up to the crow's nest. No sensation at all. In fact I never noticed the deck's antics. Dick and I had a lot of pictures to take up there and we took them. Hope they turn out good.

Aug. 1, 1927.

Here it is August and still at sea. We arrive Friday night the sixth. Shot a half roll this morn on the quarterdeck. Dick and I opened the breech of an "archie" because we thought the plug was out. It was not and we could not figure how the devil it went shut. The gunner's mate came up and showed us in detail. Very nice chap. So we learned about "archies" from him. There are a whole lot of guns on this boat. I saw a list of the munitions we are taking back with us. Ahem!

Aug. 4, 1927.

A Filipino died outside our door last night. Sure is good to be getting near home. Lots of sea gulls this morning. We're running abreast the Ore. Coast.

Aug. 5, 1927.

Dick is almost beside himself with the suspense. Jerry is getting that dreamy look in his eyes again. I'm not so calm myself. Went up in the crow's nest this morning, futile attempt.

Aug. 6, 1927.

We pull in tonight. This fog is awful. We almost hit Port Townsend because of it. Ships all around us. Seems like a ghost sea. Cannot see midships from the bridge. Thank the Lord there's Bremerton.

Puget Sound, near Bremerton, Washington;
photograph by L. Ron Hubbard

Olympic Mountains, Washington State;
photograph by L. Ron Hubbard

CHAPTER THREE

MONTANA DIARIES

Montana Diaries

U PON COMPLETION OF HIS FIRST PACIFIC PASSAGE, RON returned to the home of his grandparents in Montana for two restless semesters at the local high school. He attended classes in a white-spired edifice vaguely resembling a rectory. He joined the student newspaper staff of *The Nugget* and penned a humor column. He studied

piano with an aunt until it was discovered he could not read a single note, but rather excelled as a machine gunner with the 163rd Infantry of the Montana National Guard. He scraped together the purchase price for an old Model T roadster, accompanied a basement band on his well-traveled sax and otherwise attempted to reacclimatize to a small-town existence he had plainly outgrown.

But if China was a fabulous puzzle box, he knew very well he had only examined the first intriguing drawer. And so from these days—or more precisely from aboard the vessel on which he finally escaped provincial life—comes this account of his hurried departure and the start of a second Asian voyage, at the age of seventeen. ■

Below
Ron's "Mighty Ford" roadster and piratical pals costumed for Helena's Vigilante Day Parade; photographs by L. Ron Hubbard

Left The redoubtable marksman with the 163rd Infantry of the Montana National Guard, 1928

```
PROPERTY
OF
RONALD HUBBARD
736 - Fifth Avenue
Helena, Montana
```

I had been back in the States nearly a year. School had been hard for me and with spring turning the fields blue and green, it was all the more difficult for me to sit at a desk and work tedious Algebra problems. I counted the months of captivity that stretched before and wondered whether or not I'd require a keeper before vacation.

The long counted upon Vigilante Day had arrived. Although I did not know it, it was a period as far as school was concerned.

The parade came in the morning on that fourth of May. All Helena turned out to watch the cowboys and cavalrymen, clowns and floats file up Main St. And what characters there were. Old Henry Plummer, George Ives, Piano Jim, Custer, Jake Hoover all were to be noted.

The three girls and three boys who constituted my crowd were "Old Meg," "Betsy," "Darlin'," Harry Morgan, Captain Kidd and Captain Blood. Pirates! Of the Spanish Main, armed to the teeth and flaunting a challenge in the faces of the vigilantes.

The gayety of the day died down at last. The girls were escorted home in my mighty Ford (vintage, 1914) and my two friends were going home with me. As we sailed along, a baseball nearly bashed in my brains. I started out to chastise the offender and netted four broken metacarpals in my right hand.

That was the beginning and the end. I couldn't write and school faded from the picture. My hand was reset four times and life lost its joy. I sold the Ford and went West, taking Horace Greeley's advice.

I felt better in Seattle. Summer had already come although it was only May. I have a scout record in Seattle and took advantage of it by going to Camp Parsons on the Sound where the first period had begun.

I was happy about a week. The kids in Camp were a jolly lot and they tagged me around like a bunch

The staff of Helena High School's *Nugget* newspaper (Ron, center, second row from top)

Left "As we sailed along, a baseball nearly bashed in my brains. I started out to chastise the offender and netted four broken metacarpals in my right hand."—LRH

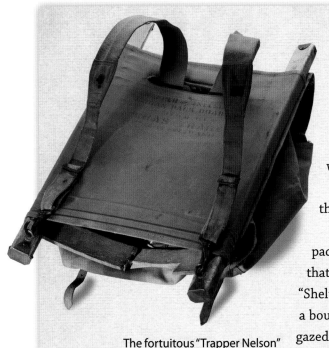

The fortuitous "Trapper Nelson" backpack that saved him from grievous injury after slipping from a precipice in the "lofty, virgin" Olympic Mountains

of dogs. Then they left and a larger crowd came. Too large for me. Besides, I was out of a job. Then, too, there is a sign in the roomy mess hall at Parsons which states: Something lost behind the ranges.

That declaration puzzled me once more. It had in the days gone by but now I was determined to find "it."

I set out at noon, hiking a swift pace under a heavy pack through the lofty, virgin Olympics. At nine o'clock that night, I made camp about two miles down trail from "Shelter Rock." Twelve hours later, I was limp on top of a boulder pile, saved from a broken spine by my pack. I gazed at the blood jumping from my wrist and decided it was high time I went to visit Herr Docteur.

While I was in Bremerton, seeing a Navy Doctor about my wrist, I learned that the "Henderson" was leaving for Guam on the first of July. It was then the twenty-fourth.

At eleven that night, I was speeding southward on the Shasta Limited California bound.

From all reports, the "Henderson" was supposed to be in San Francisco on the twenty-sixth. But when I arrived and went to the Transport Dock, she was gone. I had a bare twenty dollars in my pocket.

With a precious nickel, I purchased a newspaper and upon turning to the Shipping Section, was informed that the "President Pierce" was tied to Dock 28. At two o'clock I was standing in line at Dock 28 waiting to sign on the ship's papers as an ordinary seaman. China or bust—now had a very sinister aspect.

A happy thought struck me as I stood there ruining my nerves with a cigarette. Why not call the Twelfth Naval District and inquire after the "Henderson." Perhaps she was in San Diego. I called and found my hunch correct.

At two thirty, my trunk checked through to Diego, I was on a bus speeding southward once more.

In San Diego, faint from lack of sleep and food, I requested transportation from Captain Adams of the "Henderson." It was all right as far as he was concerned but it seemed that I needed an approval from Washington.

In search of the approval, still tired and hungry, I called on the aide to the commandant. He was very pleasant and radioed immediately. With that attended to I rented a very cheap room and slept eighteen hours in a row.

Right "China or bust"—LRH, 1928

USS *Henderson,* aboard which Ron embarked on his second Asian adventure, 1928

The morning of the next day saw a young red-headed fellow passing in and out of phone booths every few minutes. It was the thirtieth and the "Henderson" was sailing the morning of the first.

I counted my scant change and decided on some hot cakes. They seemed the cheapest and the most filling.

My message arrived the evening of the thirtieth and stated that my father's permission was needed. It ordinarily took two days to get an answer from Guam and this was no exception. The radio from my Dad arrived the morning of the first, about an hour before the "Henderson" sailed.

The evening of the thirtieth brought the sad news that my trunk was somewhere between Frisco and Diego, to be rescued a year later.

The "Henderson" sailed with me aboard. My possessions were: two handkerchiefs, two suits, one pair shoes, one worn suit, one thin topcoat, one toothbrush, two pair socks and two pennies.

No wardrobe, no money, but that trip was the best I ever took and the best I ever hope to take.

Right Asia bound, 1928

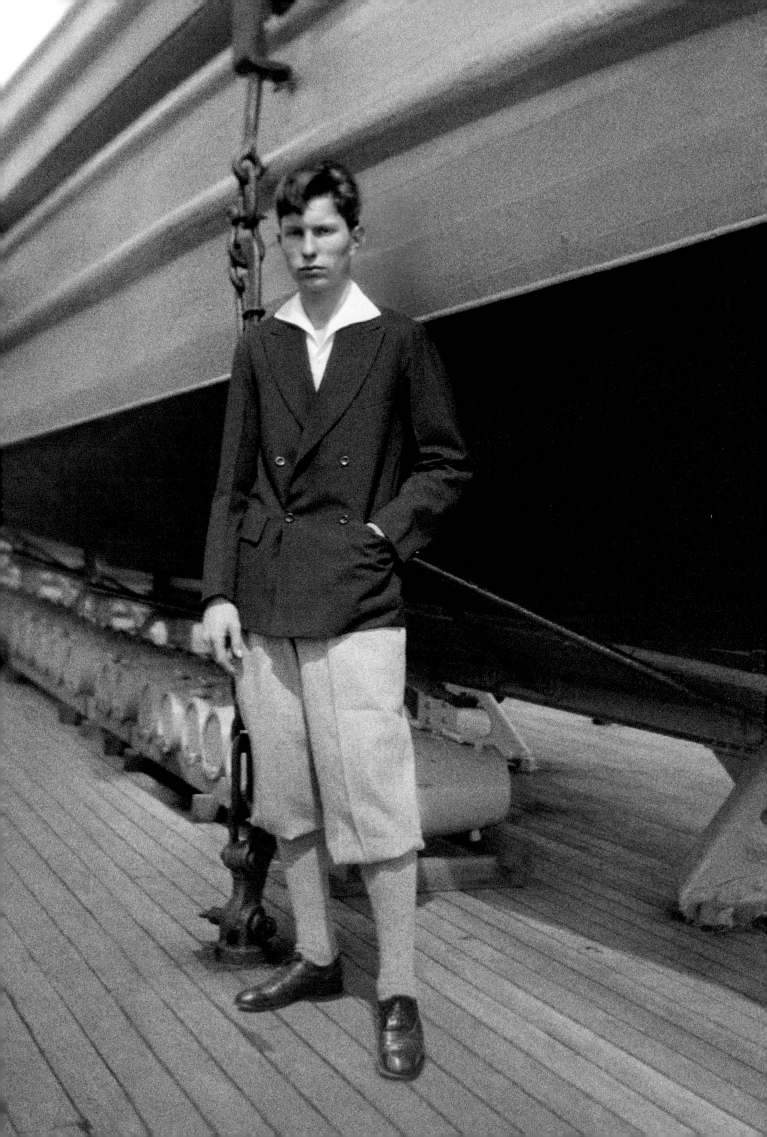

China, 1928: "Far from the sacrilegious bustle of Peking"—LRH; photograph by L. Ron Hubbard

CHAPTER FOUR

The Second
ASIAN JOURNAL

The Second
Asian Journal

THE SECOND ASIAN JOURNEY—SOME EIGHTEEN MONTHS IN duration and well off the tourist track—commenced in the spring of 1928, or not long after Ron's seventeenth birthday. In contrast to the first, he traveled alone, or in the company of such extraordinary figures as the last in the line of Royal Magicians from the court of Kublai Khan and the regional head of Her Majesty's Secret Service. Also in contrast to the first, he traveled very deep, effectively to the heart of a genuinely startling China. From his intermittent journal, much of it literally penned at sea or on the road, come his notes in the wake of high winds on the China Sea, impressions from Peking and the fabled Great Wall.

By way of a few supplementary notes, let us add the following: he actually reached the China coast after signing aboard a working schooner bound for the Malay Peninsula; hence, the description of a wind-sheared mast in typhoon weather. From the coast, he moved inland by military transport with a rail pass secured from a nameless American quartermaster. If his notes on local tourist attractions strike us as somewhat caustic, we must understand what China suffered for those monuments to royal frivolity. Then, too, this was all the China the typical tourist ever saw and he felt it a pity.

His notes from beyond the "rubberneck stations" are likewise significant. Those left to die from exposure on the platforms, for example, were most probably from Nationalist

regiments then at war with both Soviet-backed Communists and Japanese-backed warlords. In reference to the Communists comes his very pointed observation regarding the principal target of Communist propaganda, i.e., the coolie who wishes only a full belly "that he may sleep comfortably all night." In reference to collaborating warlords comes his comment regarding Chang-Tso-Lin, blown to bits in a railway carriage when his Japanese masters no longer found him useful. Chen Shek is, of course, Chiang Kai-shek, eventual rival of Communist demagogue Mao Zedong and myopic leader of the Kuomintang or Nationalist contingent. LRH references to Japanese brutality are also well taken—and all the more so, given what China would further endure through the Second World War. ■

May 30, At Sea.

Talk about luck! Last night, we had a decided falling off of the barometer. About midnight, just as I went on watch, the typhoon broke. Powerless to do anything, we all held on while the old boat sunfished.

All we could do was hold on because we were rolling 45°.

Water boiled in the scuppers, threw itself over the bow. All ports were battened down as were the hatches.

An hour after the thing started, we heard, between the intermittent screams of the wind through the tortured rigging, a resounding crackle and then a heavy bump on the deck.

The typhoon played with us until three o'clock before the torrents of driving rain became less. Then the wind began to abate.

At dawn, the world was warm and radiant. Light fleecy cirrus clouds scudded on the horizon. The sea was like glass.

But My God! The upper mast was gone, water buckets were scattered on the deck, the radio antenna and its auxiliary trailed over the side into the blue water, wire lay over everything.

3:30 o'clock.

We're 2 hours and a half late because of the typhoon but that same typhoon demands that we turn out all hands and work for about 4 days on this mess.

The only work which Ed, Ray and I will have to do will take an hour. We have to swing the aerial after the masts are put in order. It's a snap.

We are packing up now to take up our residence in the native hotel ashore. It will be sport indeed.

En route to China aboard the *Mariana Maru*, a 116-ton working schooner

Nov. 11, 1928
At Sea.

I have just returned from Peking, the civil center of old China.

The train service is pretty awful as troops commandeer them so often and their supply of rolling stock is practically nil.

Before the soldiers of Chang-Tso-Lin retreated from Peking, the service was fairly good from Tsingtao to Peking by rail, but now, the soldiers retreating from Tsinan (gee-nan) have blown up a section of a bridge on that line and the service now runs from Taku Bar through Tientsin to Peking, a distance of 185 K. which usually takes at least 16 hours.

Peking itself is fairly interesting though it duplicates itself innumerable times.

At this time of year Peking is very chilly and dust is commencing to settle thickly over everything. The winters there are very dry and cold with little snow but a great deal of ice.

The American people there are few but with the members of other consuls, the white population is decidedly greater than Guam. Gossip is snatched upon and enlarged and "fast" though they are, they love to shock themselves with the supposed depredations of someone else.

"Sept. 1928: picture of party at Dowager Empress of China's Marble Boat on lake in front of Summer Palace outside Peking, China. Among the individuals were Lt. H. R. Hubbard, Mrs. H. R. Hubbard, son L. R. Hubbard, Chief Nurse USN Hannah Workman, rickshaw coolie 'Happy,' etc."—LRH

The rubberneck stations of the tourists are:

(1) The Lama Temple

The temples number 16 inner buildings, all very much on the same order. One contains a "God" 75 feet high and carved out of one solitary cypress tree.

The people worshiping beat a drum and play a bass horn to accompany their singing. The entire place was miserably cold and very shabby. (This temple closed by order nat'l gov't. on Nov 9, 1928.) The western hills are filled with these very same temples.

(2) The Summer Palace

A decaying witness to frivolity. $50,000,000 were given the Empress Dowager by the people to construct a Chinese navy. Evidently in those days, to be honest was to be dishonorable for the Empress immediately drew up plans for a palace which was built about ten miles outside the city of Peking and named the "Summer Palace." To build it she used the money donated to build a navy. When it was finished, she had about $5,000,000 left. She used this to construct a marble ship which now floats (to all supposition) on the surface of a lake in the Palace grounds.

Now the fact of the matter is, that temple or palace was never worth over $5,000,000 all furnished with guards hired and servants paid. $5,000,000 would have been about $4,000,000 too much. The boat, a haywire contraption, with stone rudders and side wheels and capstan, never cost over $5,000 all furnished. (It is now used as a tea pavilion.) What happened to the rest of the money? She fooled the taxpayers and then fooled her courtiers and put the rest of the money in her jeans.

The palace is very spacious but very cheap as to workmanship. It has been pretty well looted by the Japanese and it is now unkempt and forlorn. It outlasted its mistress a bare 20 years.

(3) Temple of Heaven

A series of smaller temples denoting the progress of man after death. Very gaudy and more or less crudely done.

(4) The Forbidden City

There are four parts to this. One is the old royal court which is a series of buildings increasing in importance as they decrease in size. These were the reception places of generals when they came to see the Emperor every morning. Three of them are the residence places of royalty. They appear to have been very stiff and uncomfortable.

Peking, 1928; photograph by L. Ron Hubbard

Hall of Supreme Harmony, Forbidden City, China, 1928; photograph by L. Ron Hubbard

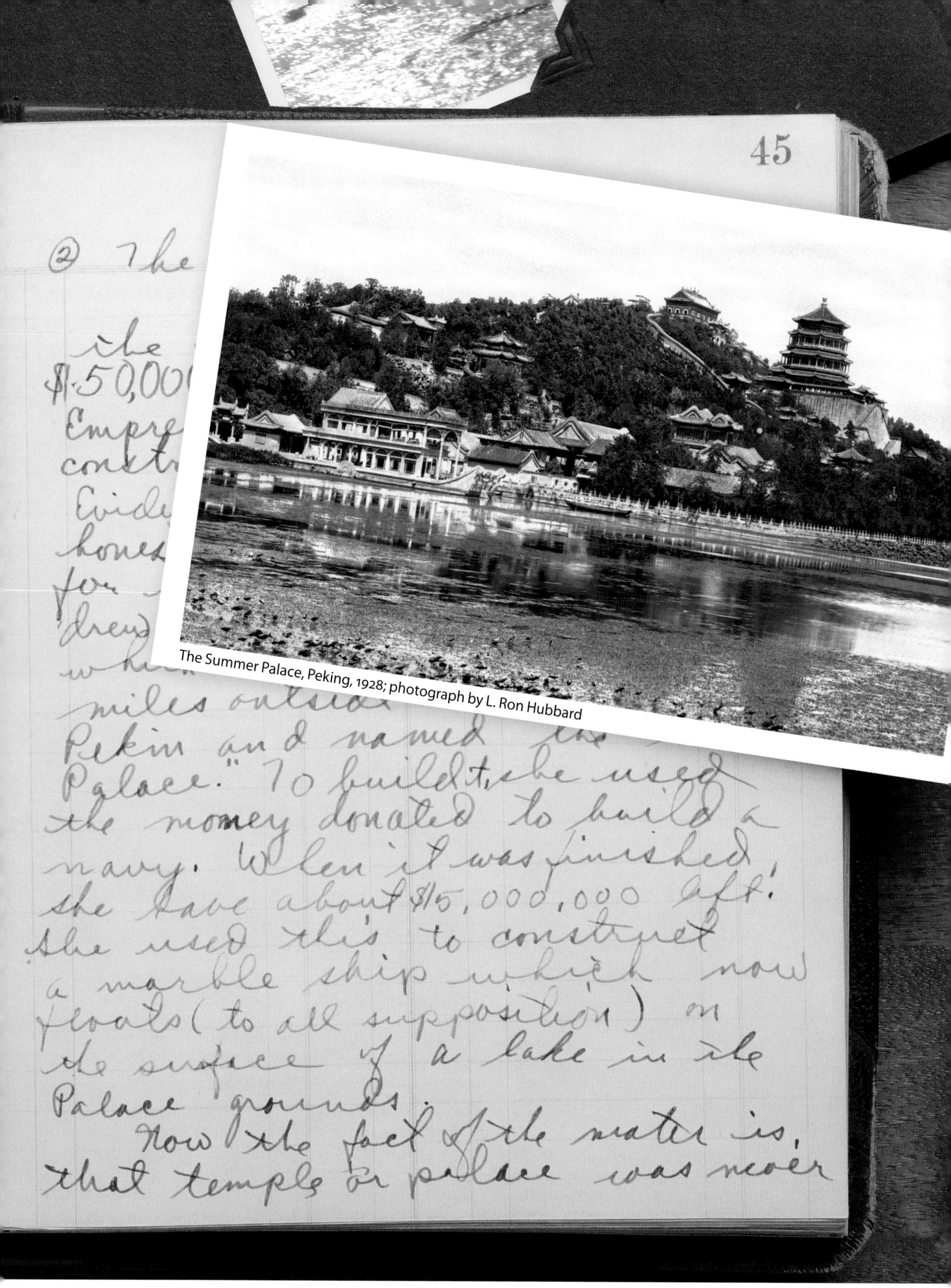

② The

the
$150,00
Empre
constr
Evide
hones
for
'drew
whic
miles outsid
Pekin and named
Palace." To build the used
the money donated to build a
navy. When it was finished,
she have about $15,000,000 left!
She used this to construct
a marble ship which now
floats (to all supposition) on
the surface of a lake in the
Palace grounds.
Now the fact of the matter is,
that temple or palace was never

The Summer Palace, Peking, 1928; photograph by L. Ron Hubbard

Entrance to the Forbidden City;
photograph by L. Ron Hubbard

Another part is the residence of the young imprisoned Emperor who was considered a menace to the Republic. The young man is now living with the Japanese at Tientsin. He is 21 years of age. His quarters in Peking were very trashy looking though they must have cost a great deal. They were infested with clocks. Every series of buildings had a couple dozen clocks within. The young Emperor took a wife in 1925 and they still share their exile.

The other two parts are not worth mentioning as they are merely more quarters of the royalty.

(5) The Winter Palace

This is not much of a palace in my estimation but the grounds are marvelous though now unkempt.

(6) The Great Wall of China

The only work of man's hand visible from Mars. Come on all of you mountaineers and put on all of your cliff climbing equipment if you want to see the wall.

This wall is very hard to reach. The railroad goes through Nan-k'ou Pass (a most marvelous railroad) and the wall extends both ways from the track to an enormous height. The wall here is 2,600 feet above sea level.

The description is somewhat misleading because it speaks of the walk to the top as being 15 minutes in length. It is an hour's hard climb to the place I went.

(7) Confucius Temple

This is more commonly known as the "Hall of Classics." It is a forest of great stone slabs which are erected in commemoration of those men who passed the examination on the "Book of Confucius" which contains 800,000 phrases, all of which were memorized by a student.

There is a throne in the central building in which the Emperor crowned was made to study. He had a different garb for every motion of his hands it seems.

"The average coolie does not even know who is hiring the soldiers who make him behave"—LRH;
photograph by L. Ron Hubbard

All these stone slabs are placed on the backs of stone turtles and other worshiped denizens of the animal world, as in the "Lama Temple" a great wooden hippopotamus stood ready to snap at trespassers.

All these places were surrounded by supposedly insurmountable walls and wide, deep moats, besides inner walls and moats. I overheard a remark to the effect that "all these kings were sure afraid of their necks."

But the grandeur of China and even the smoothness of government has departed with the emperors. Then they had unrest, it is true, but to offset it they had peace. Now they have both unrest and war. The average coolie does not know what it is all about anyway. He does not even know who is hiring the soldiers who make him behave.

"The smoothness of government has departed with the emperors. Now they have both unrest and war."—LRH; photograph by L. Ron Hubbard

I saw and admired the "Rockefeller Foundation" in Peking. It is grandly built and painted in intricate designs. But according to the residents of Peking, Rockefeller was foolish to spend $10,000,000 on such an institution. According to them, he is cutting off the only safety valves China has for her ever increasing population; i.e.: disease, sickness, and flood menace.

Even the great general "Chen Shek" has one idea that cannot be dislodged but his methods are wrong and he cannot get far enough away from his three principles to change his methods. He is having his thoughts done in blue all over the Imperial red walls of Peking. But the average coolie knows not what the characters say nor does he care. He is too interested in getting his belly full that he may sleep comfortably all night.

The very nature of the Chinaman holds him back. If his fellow should fall, John thinks it quite proper that he stamp on the underdog's face.

On a battlefield, after a battle and the retreating force has left its dead unburied and its wounded to be captured, the opposing army goes among the fallen with a free bayonet and finishes up friend and foe alike. Those that are unfortunate enough to have a rifle burst in their hands or to stop a bullet are shipped away and dumped upon a railway platform to die of their wounds or cold and starvation.

Peking camels, 1928: "A very mean breed but they resist cold"—LRH; photograph by L. Ron Hubbard

Even the Japanese are monsters as, during the Tsinan affair, the Japanese caught the Chinese Minister to Japan and cut off his nose and ears and then killed him. I had not expected such barbarism of the Japanese. And then too it was the Japanese who dynamited Chang-Tso-Lin's train.

Peking is not a very pleasant place to live. Every year about October, their winter sets in and remains seated until May, without any moisture at all. The dust becomes ankle deep in the roads and gets into everything. It causes a "Peking sore throat" which lasts all winter. It becomes very cold and skating is the order of the day. Every one of the legations has a private rink; all the tennis courts are transformed into ice ponds.

I believe that the most startling thing one can see in Northern China is the number of camels. These are of a very mean breed but they resist cold and carry burdens which is all the Chinaman requires of them. Everyday in Peking one can see many caravans in the streets. They have a very stately shamble. They carry their head high; their mean mouths wagging and their humps lolling from side to side. All my life I have associated camels with Arabs and it strikes a discordant note within me to see the beasts shepherded by Chinamen.

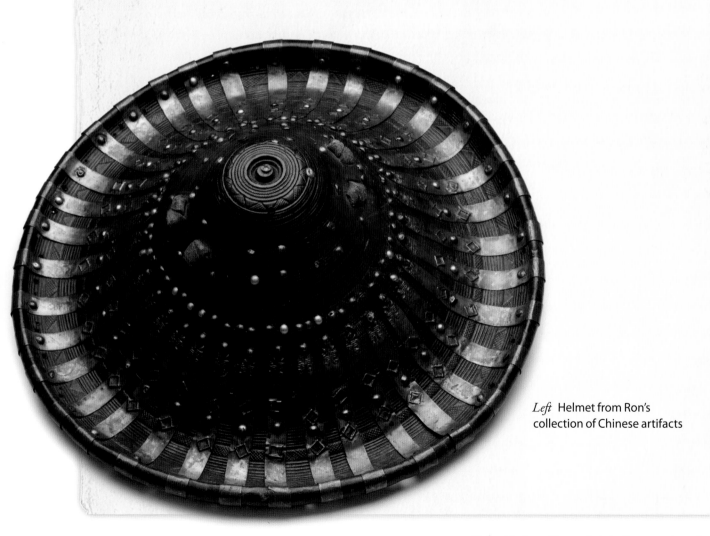

Left Helmet from Ron's collection of Chinese artifacts

Right Mariana Maru sails into the sunset, 1928; photograph by L. Ron Hubbard

The Great Wall

From a slightly later journal, most probably the spring of 1929, comes Ron's etched impressions from a two-thousand-foot precipice along the Great Wall. The entry is particularly significant for the subsequent LRH photograph from these same ramparts. Capturing a full seven turns of the legendary wall, the shot would eventually amaze readers of National Geographic and various high-school texts. ∎

The plains of Mongolia stretch bleakly, forbidding, yet beckoning, backed again and again by the Great Wall. Granite mountains turn their craven faces to the grey sky and the wind-god chaps their cheeks with icy blasts. The ages past, there stand to await oblivion which never comes. Nothing but thorns and breeding nothing but dust, reminisces the men who have trod before never to trod again.

Far from the sacrilegious bustle of Peking, out of earshot, and eyeshot too, of civilization, I slipped a cautious hand about the watchtower's window and with a last strain of muscle, lifted my body through, to gasp at the approximity of the world's end. The rest of the blockhouse was not there. Dripping from every pore, I curled myself on the broad, lofty ledge and closed my swimming eyes.

I had climbed for a long, long time over the sharp granite rock chips, which tore my futile shoes to threads. I had burst through tawny thorn trees, onward and upward from Nan-k'ou. The Great Wall was everywhere, but for me, there was only the highest pinnacle.

I opened my eyes and viewed my conquest. The Wall straggled miles before me, broken in places, cut here and there by the sandstorms.

Twisting and turning, even writhing, in the distance, keeping alive the memory of China's glorious past.

The wind whipped through my hair and stung my cheeks with its bitter breath. It shrieked about the lonely tower, screamed to frighten me away from its playthings, the Wall, the mountains and the thorns. And I laughed to match its wildness and opened my blue shirt at the throat to flaunt the wind-god and ridicule his power.

But the laugh died presently, the wall was too stern and frowning. *Ron*

"The Wall straggled miles before me, broken in places, cut here and there by the sandstorms"—LRH; photograph by L. Ron Hubbard

Left The Great Wall, above Nan-k'ou Pass, China, 1928; photograph by L. Ron Hubbard

"The plains of Mongolia stretch bleakly, forbidding, yet beckoning, backed again and again by the Great Wall"—LRH; photograph by L. Ron Hubbard

USS *Kittery*, aboard which Ron sailed from Norfolk, Virginia, to San Juan, Puerto Rico, in 1932

CHAPTER FIVE

The CARIBBEAN LETTERS

The Caribbean Letters

IN THE AUTUMN OF 1932, A TWENTY-ONE-YEAR-OLD L. RON Hubbard set sail for the Caribbean on behalf of his father and a syndicate of fellow officers with dreams of securing precious mineral rights, particularly gold. Remembered today as the Puerto Rican Mineralogical Expedition, the venture would culminate in that island's first

Below Martinique, Lesser Antilles, 1932

complete mineralogical survey under United States protectorship. Judging from letters to family and friends, however, there were definitely other tales to be told from Puerto Rico—intense, personal and clearly touching upon questions for later exploration. To begin with, we find his summary notes from the USS *Kittery,* a none too luxurious cargo transport bound for the United States Marine Base at Guantánamo Bay and thence on to San Juan. ▪

Left An approaching storm; photograph by L. Ron Hubbard

≡━◇◇◇◇◇◇◇━≡

Aboard USS Kittery Out of Norfolk
October 26, 1932

Here we go, rapidly on our way to the horizon's foggy edge with only several seasick passengers among our few deadheads. Old Cape Charles and Cape Henry faded plumb out of sight in this nasty Virginia pea soup and that's that.

≡━◇◇◇◇◇◇◇━≡

USS Kittery High Seas
October 27, 1932

I write in a narrow little stateroom while seated on a canvas stool with the typewriter perched on the edge of a shifting bunk. I've worn the same shirt for three days and I've only shaved once. Deplorable.

≡━◇◇◇◇◇◇◇━≡

USS Kitkat
The Ocean Blue
Briny Deep Boulevard
October 29, 1932

Went out and looked at our stars a little while ago and the stars are gaining that tropical brightness. Tonight we pass San Salvador. The island with which Columbus has duped the world for a few centuries.

Same Ship
Same Sea
Same Boulevard
30 Same month.
Same old year.

Tomorrow we will be in Cap Haitien. And just as soon as we land, I'm going to have on a pair of tennis shoes, khaki pants and a sun helmet and walk right straight south and away from the ocean, the ship, and the town. I'll find me a hoss someplace and ride back through the mountains to the Citadel de Christophe. This Citadel is quite something even though it's in ruins. Cost the lives of 35,000 workmen to build and covers acres and acres of mountainside. And I'm going to tie the hoss to a banana stalk and scramble over masonry and go right on up to the topmost top of the lofty edifice. And after I get up there with the wind shrieking through my clothes and trying to rip off the strapped sun helmet, I'm going to sit down very calmly and look back across the jungles at the sea.

The Citadel de Christophe (Citadelle Laferrière) outside
Cap Haitien, 1930; photograph by L. Ron Hubbard

A Marine Named Faulkner

Having previously served with the 20th Marine Corps Reserves (and led his Company G to nineteen out of twenty silver cups in Eastern Seaboard Reserve competition), Ron was known to many a leatherneck in many a far-flung outpost. His links to the young Johnny Faulkner in this letter from Guantánamo, however, involve rather more. In speaking of Phil Browning, Ron is referencing the fellow aviator with whom he spent a barnstorming summer of 1931. In speaking of Sandino, he is referencing General Augusto César Sandino, leader of Nicaragua's 1927 anti-imperialist insurrection and thus a particularly insignificant footnote in United States military history. To put it bluntly, those like Johnny Faulkner fought and died for American banana interests. The rest is tragically self-explanatory. ∎

Guantánamo Bay, Cuba

November 1, 1932

When I stepped onto the dock with letters in my hand I found that I couldn't mail them outside the Marine camp. A corporal was standing there and he offered to mail them for me. One of them was addressed to Phil Browning. I went on up town with the chief of the shore patrol from the ship. We were suddenly hailed from the rear. The corporal was coming after us in a heat-defying trot. He waved the letter to Phil in front of my face and stated that he knew the guy. So he took me up to the Marine's Club and ordered me some beer and we sat and chewed the fat for a time. It came out then that I'd known this corporal in China. He is Johnny Faulkner.

I could see that he wanted me to tell him something and I knew that it wasn't about Phil. So I talked about Phil's sisters—Eleanor, Florence, and Carol. The last two are supposed to be twins although they don't look alike. Eleanor is married and in Spain. The twins are somewhere in the East. I talked about all three and his eyes lit up when I mentioned Caroline. Then I racked my brain and suddenly remembered that Carol had mentioned a Marine to me several times. Then I even recalled his name. It was the same one. Carol often acted half-peeved when I told her I didn't know every leatherneck that breathed. And I'd see Carol every time Phil came to Washington because he usually stayed with the twins. Carol had told me an awful lot about Faulkner. In fact, more than once, I suspected that she was in love with him.

Hours passed. Beer went down the hatch. We went up to the Marine camp and had a shower and then returned to the Club. I had told Johnny Faulkner all I knew about Carol and how she was getting on. Other times I wouldn't have bothered much. But you see, after you get acquainted with love, your understanding is sympathetic and your outlook softened quite a bit. So I talked about Carol, and he listened.

During the course of the evening, we were rudely interrupted now and then by Marines who had taken one too many, Marines who had known me here or in Timbuktu or someplace, Marines who had heard

Left San Juan, Puerto Rico, 1932; photograph by L. Ron Hubbard

about me, Marines who knew friends of mine, and Marines who wished to clarify my ideas surrounding certain instances and incidents which have to do with military men, and Marines who were Johnny's friends. Every now and then, the garçon would fetch some spots of rhum, and someone would sign a chit. They wouldn't let me pay for anything as usual. A white civilian is a sensation in Cap Haitien, a white civilian with red hair or black hair or any other kind of hair is rarely seen in the Marine's Club. Add that to the fact that I was known to most of them in one way or another, and you have the hubbub in mind. Every now and then some Marine would insult another Marine and the MPs would rally round. And every time the MPs appeared, a cry would go up for me. I'd put on a stern face of authority, the battlers would subside and the MPs salute me—of course they'd take me for an officer in civvies—and leave the place. Following such incidents, triumphs over the law as they were, the garçons would very busily trot out the rhum so that everybody could drink to my health. But they never did drink to my health. At the proposal of the toast, I'd shake my head, stand up on a chair and address the multitude in solemn tones to the effect that it was extremely necessary for everyone to drink "to something." And down the hatch the rhum would go.

And the score or so of leathernecks would squint their eyes at me for a moment and then shake their heads. "Dunno what I'm drinking to, old son, but it's oke with me." I never explained, except to Johnny.

About eight, we tired of the Club and went to a place called Anna Loos which happens to be a bar. By this time, although Johnny had said plenty, he hadn't given me a very clear idea of what it was all about. He was hiding quite a bit. I knew something was wrong because the kid is a wreck. Then, by piecing remarks together, I found his story.

Six years ago, Johnny Faulkner, Sergeant of Marines, was on duty guarding the mails between Port Huron, Mich. and Chicago. He spent the layover of his run in Port Huron, and in some way became acquainted with the Browning family who, at the time, were living there in toto. He fell in love with Carol, but with the usual Marine brusqueness, didn't tell her much about it. Didn't even mention the fact in the three words. Carol was about eighteen then, I suppose. And she never has had a great deal to say. In fact, the only time she ever really told me anything was last winter when the husband of a family she was staying with directed his rather clear and extremely unwanted attentions upon her. Then, as the best friend of her brother, I diplomatically aided her as best I could. There's a lot of diplomacy in a sock on the nose.

Johnny was on that run for several months and he must have seen a great deal of Carol. Most of the time, she just sat and listened to him while he told her about far-off places. Neither of them could have said a great deal about what they felt. He couldn't marry her because he was a Sergeant of Marines and unable to support a wife. She must have sensed this, for she said nothing. He knew this and didn't touch her. Military men are like that when they love. If impossibility arises, they say nothing. Not even to their friends.

And so the winter wore away and spring came. And with spring, the Nicaraguan elections. Sergeant Johnny went south to Nicaragua into the thick of that ugly, unwarranted, jungle war at the height of Sandino's murky career.

Johnny had a friend. Another Johnny named Kimple who was also a sergeant of the Corps. The two of them had been together their whole time in the Marines—eight years before 1926. Faulkner, because of his splendid record, was ordered to the Guardia—that body of native soldiery officered by non-commissioned officers of the Marine Corps. Kimple was made Faulkner's second lieutenant. And so Guardia Lieutenant Kimple, and Guardia Captain Faulkner started in to make things hot for Sandino. In Faulkner's locker there are eight citations won in 1926. He didn't know that I saw them.

Yes, the two of them burned up the jungles and fought all over the lot. Not for the glory at all. For the fun of it and because they were together and because they were Marines. Summer faded out, though it made no difference in the climate of hot Nicaragua.

Kimple took out a squad of native soldiers one steaming dawn and started out to trace a telegraph line. The jungle was thick on either side of the narrow trail. A few hours of heavy marching. A scrub tree spitting flame. The native sergeant led a mule back to camp. On the back of that mule, an object was covered with a white sheet. Faulkner came out of his tent and stared at the sergeant's brown face. Captain Faulkner needed to ask no questions. He fainted dead away. Kimple had been cut half in two with machine gun fire. Half on one side of the mule and half on the other.

Faulkner took the trail alone, his rifle slung under his arm, the safety catch off. They found him with half his guts shot away, his bandoleer empty of shells, the crew of the machine gun lying in lifeless heaps over their cold armament.

They brought Johnny back to the base and sewed him up. He lived and they shipped him to the hospital at San Diego. A month later he was on his way to China. He wrote to no one. Not even his family knew where he was. One general court-martial followed another. They shipped him to Haiti.

He hasn't heard from Carol since that summer nor she from him.

He has a few more years to live and he's trying his best to get them over with. He's rotting himself out with rhum and eating out his heart for Carol. He almost ceases to breathe when you're telling him about her.

But he's all shot to pieces inside, and even if he took good care of himself, the bullets which tore him up would finish their work in a short time.

Faulkner is really a gentleman ranker. He is not built from enlisted material. And even when he's drunk—which is the final test—he's a gentleman.

I know his story by putting scraps together. He started to tell me about Kimple. At first his face was calm. He dragged out a few words. Then he looked down at his feet. His hands contracted slowly, nervously. He was trying to get hold of himself again.

A man doesn't cry easily like a woman. He isn't built to cry and sobs rack his frame.

The first time in my life I ever saw a Marine give way.

They're hard stuff, for they deal with death.

Hurricane warnings were up and the Kittery was sailing at eleven. Johnny borrowed a truck from the guard and we drove down to the dock.

"Don't," said Johnny, "tell her that you saw me here."

"Of course I'm going to write to her. The kid's starving in Washington today." I hadn't told him that.

"Please don't write." Johnny rubbed his knuckles. "I know, I'll send her an anonymous allotment. But don't write. I don't want her to know where I am."

"All right, Johnny. I won't."

A fine rain was coming down and when the boat shoved away from the dock and pointed its nose at the Kittery's lights in the stream, I looked back. Johnny was still standing there. Alone. Shot to pieces. Rotting his guts with rhum. Eating his heart out for a girl he hasn't seen or heard of for five years.

And Carol, leaning forward across a dinner table, interrupting Phil's monologue, an eager expression on her face. "Ron, did you ever know a Marine named Faulkner?"

"I told you before that I didn't."

Her eyes on her plate. A little sigh which nobody ever noticed but me. *Ron*

Right USS *Kittery:* "I write in a narrow little stateroom while seated on a canvas stool with the typewriter perched on the edge of a shifting bunk"—LRH

Letters from Puerto Rico

With Ron's arrival in the Puerto Rican capital of San Juan, what he would describe as *"prospecting in the wake of the Conquistadores"* began in earnest with the sluicing of inland rivers for alluvial gold. *"It was terribly hot and we were soaking wet most of the time,"* he remarked in a later account, and all was initially for naught. In any case, and quite in addition to that later account, comes these rather more personal notes from that mining adventure. ■

San Juan, P.R.

November 11, 1932

Jesus, you should have been with me today! All over the damned island and babbling Spanish a mile a minute. Pants tucked down into laced boots, the blue-banded sun hat at a precarious angle and the old battle flag waving under the brim. And the sweat dripping from the pores as fast as Spanish from the tongue. And the dirty dusty towns with the gaping populace.

We hired two foremen today to supervise the first sluice which will be running full tilt by Sunday. Muck and gold.

You ought to see the town where I'll be bivouacked for the coming months. Corozal. Your mail will be forwarded there from San Juan, but please keep sending it to general delivery San Juan. This town is a little cluster of shiplap shacks around an ancient, moldy, and unpicturesque cathedral. The heat bubbles off the streets a mile a minute and with it come a thousand but faintly identified odors. I don't know where I'll live. Paul and Carper and Mrs. Wilkerson have their eye on a house and they think I'm going to live with them. I'm not. A mangy little hut and a courteous houseboy will be my billet. I don't like to live in close quarters with Americans in the tropics. And I enjoy lack of routine too well to have meals on time. For a while I'll camp in an excuse for a hotel and live in my working clothes.

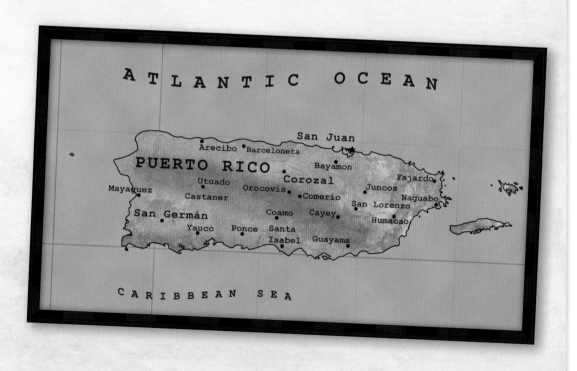

Left "Sluicing with crew on Corozal River '32 P.R."—LRH

San Juan

November 13, 1932

It rained torrents four times today. It was a cold rain and my clothes are thin and shelter did not exist. My feet were ankle deep in mud. I tried to find shelter, crawled under a rock, got wet, came out and almost drowned in the usual tropical cloudburst. Cigarettes wet, not a dry stitch on me, an hour's ride to San Juan with a breeze almost freezing my wet clothes. A cold shower. A slight dinner. A bad-tasting cigarette. This letter. And then bed, praise be to God. I only hope I wake up feeling better though I know I won't. Wish I had a great big drink. Still shivering though the thermometer is hovering around ninety.

Puerto Rican farmland, 1932;
photograph by L. Ron Hubbard

Corozal, P.R.

November 20, 1932

Down in the muck today. Way down deep. And I should be fairly contented because this is the first day of rest I've had since I arrived in Puerto Rico. Carper and Wilkerson went out yesterday to see some property and left me running the sluice. The gold on bedrock gave out at about the five dollar mark and I had to close down. Today I could have gone out and tried with a pan but I thought I'd better grab the opportunity while it presented itself as I'm pretty well fagged out.

A funeral just went by on the dirt street in front of the hotel. The wail of a clarinet, the throb of a bass horn. And several little children with flowers carrying a tiny blue casket which is probably now being lowered into the earth. Ragged people, a garish coffin—cheap. And I caught myself thinking as that little box went by, "What a lucky kid." He'll never have to combat the storm of life. He'll never know the sting of sweat, the violence of sudden rains, of muck oozing between his toes, the dirty smell of a native dwelling. He died without knowing. They die like flies in this country, children. Disease, frailty, the harshness of life.

But what if he had been a child in the States? It would have been pretty much the same story. He would have rushed through life without ever stopping to taste it.

You know, the padres tell us that there is a hell to which we will go if we do not live right here on this earth. I wonder why they stress such things when there's hell all about them right here. If we do wrong, we pay for it a thousand times over. I doubt that anyone really escapes punishment for havoc wrought. That sounds religious. Well, maybe it is. I choose to call it two-bit philosophy. There's always a nemesis right around the corner. I have a sneaking hunch right now that I've let the past come a little too close. It slaps me in the face now and then when I walk down a hot street in wet boots and feel the sun eating away at my shoulders. A puff of sizzling wind bringing odors all too familiar.

Capital Hotel
San Juan, P.R.

November 24, 1932

Today was Thanksgiving. I just finished a sketchy meal in the restaurant below. My first taste of food since six-thirty this morning, and it is now about eight-thirty at night.

All day I was with Jimmy Gresham. Tomorrow I'm moving my duffle up to his place where I will stay until the ship sails for Santo Domingo. I do not know exactly when that will be but at the most, it should be five days.

And all day long, Thanksgiving or no Thanksgiving, I was in the thick of sorrow. That's no way to spend a holiday, but somehow I didn't mind at all. You see, Jimmy's girl—Helen Nechodama, the artist—left for New York today on the S.S. Borinquen. She is going to Paris and it is extremely doubtful that she will ever come back.

You see, Jimmy loves her, and she doesn't love Jimmy. He is rather old, about forty, though he doesn't appear to be more than thirty. He is about the swellest friend I have. A gentleman through and through, always ready to help anyone out of a tough spot.

"I died today, the day she began to live." Jimmy was broken up. He went to the boat alone to see her off and came back about two in the afternoon. We heard the Borinquen whistle as she left the dock. And from Jimmy's wide verandah, three stories above the street and exposed to all the sea, we watched the ship pass El Morro and grow smaller and smaller in the distance, until at last, even her smoke was gone from the horizon. Jimmy was all shot to pieces. I mean really ill, not just sad, but vitally and physically sick. Each time he drank her health, he smashed his glass between his fingers. Blood dripped slowly from his right hand, and his knuckles were raw from pounding them against the cement wall. He didn't mind my being there, in fact, I am sure that he was glad I was.

He downed about a half a bottle of rhum before I finally coaxed him to lie down a few minutes. That was about seven o'clock. Two more stiff drinks and he was asleep. He still sleeps, I hope. I'll be there in the morning when he wakes up.

God, it was awful to see a man shatter right in front of your eyes.

He was in such terrible shape that I unloaded all the gats in the house and pocketed all the shells, locked up all the poisons in the medicine cabinet, and locked the doors onto the verandah.

Because he'll never see her again, he doesn't care about anything, now. I've seen quite a bit of various and assorted death, but never before in my life have I seen a living man die and go on living. I know now that Jimmy will never be himself again. Never again the cheerful, energetic Jimmy who is loved in Mexico, South America, and the West Indies. He won't be James Robert Gresham again. I'm so glad that I can help him if only for a few days.

The San Juan central plaza: "I'll camp in an excuse for a hotel and live in my working clothes"—LRH

Corozal, P.R.

December 21, 1932

This place is such a madhouse of noise that I haven't been able to put two collective thoughts together since I came. You see, a gambler is living in the same room with me, and as he was here first, I haven't any room to put my stuff away or get a desk in place. Just a few minutes ago I conceived the brilliant idea of putting a dresser drawer upside down on my bed and using that as a desk. What a country!

One doesn't mind having to do without things if he can do without them quietly, but when he has noise and crowding thrown in on top of it he's in a pretty bad way.

God knows which way things are going to turn now. Wilky and I are going to start shipping ore pretty soon, but Carper is still hanging on to the money and it's a guess when he'll let loose of the stuff. Until that time we are rooted to hotels with unpaid bills. I left a trunk at the Capital and asked Axmeyer the owner to wait for his dough. He cried loud and long, but that's that.

I laughed loud and long the other night over a frog that happened into the hotel and made all the ladies scramble up on chairs and the men look stern and strong. I laughed until I found out I couldn't stop. Realized then it was the first time in a long, long while. Sense of humor must be deserting me for a bit.

Yesterday I went up to visit an Americano named Grathwohl. He lost a fortune here in the last hurricane and now his creditors are all hounding him and he's built himself a little shack on his ranch where he grows fruit. The shack has a bedroom, a kitchen, a living room and a porch, and though it's as rugged as the devil, it's still a lot more like home than any native shack around here. Grathwohl came down and picked me up at this "hotel" and then we went up and cooked lunch over a kerosene stove. After Spanish beans and rice, the fried pork, baked beans, pilot biscuit, and new spuds sure tasted grand. After lunch we went down to the river which runs through Grath's land and looked things over. He has many different kinds of minerals on his place: Copper, gold, silver, lead, iron, and manganese, though none of them in any great quantity. The river had overflowed its banks due to a storm of the past evening and black sand was deposited in the rocks and grass along the banks. We shot the breeze for some time and panned the dirt we dug out of small crevasses. And when we cleaned up, we had over a dollar's worth of gold! That's phenomenal for this country. So we weighed it out nicely and I sold my half for fifty-two cents to the local druggist. So we have cigarette money at least and we can mail this letter. After we had supper we came back to the hotel and played blackjack for several hours. For matches as everybody is broke. I was theoretically two thousand dollars in the hole midway through the game but I came out a thousand dollars the winner. All of which must be intensely interesting.

Grath's wife is in the States, as he lost his big home here and most of his dough. There's a pal for you. Sticks about as close as a drunken Irishman. Everything lovely as long as Grath makes dough and can support her in the style to which she is accustomed. But when the servants are no more and the maple turns into pine flooring and the bath is outside, the rat leaves the sinking ship. What a pal. And Grath feels remorseful because he seduced his house girl a while back. He says he's gone tropical and can't help it. Of course, he excuses his wife and doesn't even mention her defection, but it's damned obvious.

Corozal, Puerto Rico: "At least once a day some major crime would dart forth to amaze the populace"—LRH

San Germán

February 6, 1933

Here I am in San Germán sampling and surveying the Torres mine. Mucho trabajo. Anyway, only a kilometer away lives a very winsome muchacha in a hacienda grande. But, even though I could live there like a king, have horses or anything I needed, I'm sitting in a lousy, ramshackle hotel. The moon is beautiful outside, too.

Surveying mine tunnels and playing hopscotch over hundred foot shafts whilst swatting big spiders and dodging flying cockroaches literally and figuratively has driven me to drink.

Routine these days is quite without routine. Walk miles, ride kilometers, scramble over rotten logs, forget about lunch, remember at dark that one must sleep someplace. Tired and punch-drunk and goofy. What a life?!

We'll know within a hair of what we have here within six weeks from today. If there's nothing to warrant development of any of this stack of options I've accumulated, it's heigh-ho! And away we go. Mañana is another day.

Ron's well-worn mining pans for extracting alluvial gold

WEST INDIES MINERALS
INCORPORATED
MINERS AND EXPORTERS
MANGANESE, SILICA, GLASS SAND, GOLD, SILVER, LEAD, COPPER
MARBLE, ONYX, MAGNESITE, IRON ORE, BRICK CLAY, ZINC

MINES
ISLAND OF PUERTO RICO

WASHINGTON, D. C.
BENJAMIN FRANKLIN STATION BOX 302

OPERATIONS OFFICE
SAN JUAN, P. R.

30 March 1933

Mr. L. Ron Hubbard
West Indies Minerals
Puerto Rico

Dear Mr. Hubbard:

Due to the recent developments in the investigations of the deposits and properties under consideration on the island it is imperative that you return to Washington for a conference.

You will leave Puerto Rico on the first available transportation for New York and thence to Washington, D.C.

Such funds as are now on hand and in excess of your transportation requirements will be made available to the corporation's engineer to defray his expenses until the 8th of April and his transportation to the States should it become advisable for him to return at that date.

It is requested that you provide yourself with all available samples and data on the silica, manganese, marble, onyx and gold or any other product that might be marketable.

Yours truly;
West Indies Minerals, Inc.

A Postscript from Corozal

Bet you think I'm an awful aircastle constructionist. Well, I at least try to make things come true, and you'll never shoot the moon by aiming at China. The higher you attempt, the higher you'll get in the end.

Right now I'm believing that the fates have been foiled in their design to make a certain redhead settle down like a nice boy and become as standard as the next-door neighbor! There's nothing but work in this world. Nothing but work and grief and routine! Oh yeah? Well, I'm just young enough to call the guy that says that a liar. Maybe the sad truth will come to us in the end, but think what a fine time we're going to have finding that truth out!

L. Ron Hubbard

Right The mining crew; photograph by L. Ron Hubbard

CHAPTER SIX

Letter from the INTERIOR

Letter from the
Interior

QUITE IN ADDITION TO WHAT THIS PUERTO RICAN Mineralogical Expedition provided by way of sheer adventure, Ron's passage across the island would further prove altogether significant in terms of his greater journey. In particular, he would speak of his stay among the classically rustic *jibaro*. Generally scattered along the

Puerto Rican interior, the *jibaro* are said to represent all that is both pure and mysterious within Caribbean people. Their faith is an exotic blend of Catholicism and indigenous animism described as *espiritismo* and involving a cosmology of many thousand natural spirits. The classic LRH tale of primeval haunting, *Fear,* was partially inspired by what he witnessed among these people, as was much subsequent ethnological research. But in either case, as he elsewhere wrote, "There's something here to know."

From the heart of this curious interior comes the deeply reflective letter to a friend from December 9, 1932. Precisely what prompted the letter is unclear, but the questions he poses would prove important, and his sense of life as all too brief says much about what drove him to live several lives through the next dozen years. Also significant is the underlying sense of futility at this sobering juncture when, as he later put it, "I fell off the cliff" of known knowledge relating to the human condition. ■

Left Mouth of an abandoned mineshaft: "We go upon the theory that it was not possible for the Spaniards to have exhausted the entire mineral wealth of the islands"—LRH

Puerto Rico

December 9, 1932

Days creep out and out into a long stream of never-ending thought and hope. Long gray days at contrast from one another only through mood. Long days beset by minor plots and lost action. Milling, loose days.

Something has happened way down inside me. Something has gone only to be replaced with something infinitely more precious. The whole world has changed. The sunsets have a different color, faces wear a different expression, thoughts follow different channels.

God knows I know little enough about life. Never have I realized the things to be learned under this uneven fabric of mixed byplays. There's more to life than living. Just as there's more to thought than thinking. Life is a tapestry fashioned out of dreams. And though the pattern is without pattern, and the design without plot, there is a beauty through it all which one comes to understand only through the realization of inability to understand.

Thousands on life's road behind us have cast puzzled eyes to calm stars, and raising their dust-dried mouths out of the swirl around them, have cried out in weary, wondering tones "What is life?" Each man sees a difference. No one can solve to universal satisfaction this most wondrous of puzzles.

There are the fools of us who try. Who try only to have their voice thrown back at them through the years and realize that that which is settled for today has changed for the morrow. And there are those of us who escape by refusing to utter the cry. Who enclose ourselves in a self-centered, unsympathetic shell. But they too have their hopes and dreams altered, their wants destroyed, their desires supplanted. Nothing is ever settled forever, for who are we but puny men facing an unknown a million times greater and countless billions of years older than ourselves.

For how can we understand that outside us when we can barely realize that which goes on within? Moles digging through time, a halting, hesitant creeping forward, with time, under us as a roadway, sweeps back with pictures we call the past. Motionless monuments never again to be touched. Still, dead moments never again to be revived. The brightness of sunshine, the grayness of tears, frozen together, dead forever along the roadway of time.

But after all, there is still the germ of motion in this infinite smallness called the present. Life is not long. It does not stretch out before us or flutter as a pennon behind us. It is the hazily bound instant, unbelievably brief which we call the present. It is the moment, the perpetual moment which seems to stand still all around us while we sip from its cup.

And these moments are deserting us one by one. Piling themselves from our aura to stand at attention behind us. How we waste them!

That is my philosophy of time. It must also be the philosophy of youth, for otherwise I would not presume to dub such mutterings as philosophy at all. But there is the reason for the way I try to live, and there, I believe is the chart by which you gauge yourself. Hurry! Hurry! Hurry! The moments are fleeting. They are slipping away from us. Soon we will die. We will no longer raise our eyes to the stars and cry out the question. Our lips will no longer touch the rim of the cup. Then we too will stand at attention in the path of time. Pitiful, inanimate little figures. Dead and soon forgotten no matter the heights the world has given us in their calendar of fame. The pages of that calendar are often turned and few there are who move with the page.

Hurry! Hurry! There's no time to lose. No time for lengthy preparations. Our platforms are so frail, our importance so small, our immortality so unassured. The instants fleet. Speed and the instants are saved a few at a time. Live fast and you live long. No time for empty dreaming. No time for useless building. But only time to live and taste the wine of living. No time to be afraid. No time to waste on worry. Only the moment, for that is the only thing in life worth saving. *Ron*

Another view of a land where "Life is a tapestry fashioned out of dreams"—LRH; photograph by L. Ron Hubbard

"It is the horizon one never sees which lures him"
—LRH, South Pacific, 1927

Epilogue

A WORD OF ADVICE
TO A FELLOW ADVENTURER

He who would look forward into time

cannot but shudder at the prospect of the future.

But I have lived through yesterday.

I am living through today.

Why should I fear to live through tomorrow?

L. RON HUBBARD

APPENDIX

GLOSSARY

A

abate: diminish or reduce in intensity, amount, etc. Page 67.

able-bodied: having a strong, healthy body; physically fit. Page 42.

aboard, signing: writing one's name on (something) for the purposes of identification or authorization, specifically, in being hired as crew aboard (on) a ship. Page 65.

abode: a place where one lives or stays; home. Page 38.

abreast: in a position parallel to or alongside of something stationary (used when referring to something that is directly to the side as one travels on a ship). Page 48.

abstaining from: choosing deliberately not to use or do something. Page 14.

accordion: a portable wind instrument having a large bellows (a device for producing a strong current of air by expanding and contracting) that forces air through small metal reeds, a keyboard for the right hand and buttons for sounding single notes with the left hand. Page 39.

Acey Deucey: a variation of the game of *backgammon,* a board game for two players who each move their fifteen pieces around the board according to the throw of a pair of dice. Page 43.

ado: doing, action, business or fuss. Page 34.

adolescent: lacking wisdom or emotional development normally associated with adults. Page 3.

aerial: also called *antenna,* a metallic piece of equipment used in the sending and receiving of radio signals. Page 67.

Agana: former name of *Hagatna,* the capital of Guam, located on the western coast of the island. Page 34.

Agat: a village on the southwest coast of the island of Guam. Page 40.

aguardiente: a strong alcoholic liquor, such as originally made in Spain. From Spanish *agua,* water and *ardiente,* fiery. Page 38.

ahem!: used in writing to indicate the sound of a quiet cough, humorously expressing surprise or disapproval, to attract attention or the like. Page 48.

ailed: affected with an unnamed pain or discomfort (physical or emotional); troubled. Page 3.

aircastle constructionist: someone who builds air castles. An *air castle* (or *castle in the air*) is a fanciful or impractical idea or hope; daydream. Page 102.

albeit: although; even if. Page vii.

algebra: a branch of mathematics in which symbols, usually letters of the alphabet, are used to represent unknown numbers. Page 55.

alligator pears: another term for *avocados,* fruit with a leathery, dark-green or blackish skin with a soft, smooth-tasting, pale-green flesh and a large stony seed, eaten raw. Page 43.

allotment: the payment of part of one's wages to a specified person. Page 90.

alluvial: found in *alluvium,* a deposit of soil formed in river valleys from material washed down by the river. Page 92.

Americano: Spanish for a person from North America, used here in reference to the United States. Page 98.

ancillary: supplying something additional, such as data or information. Page 9.

and then some: and much more in addition. Page 46.

animism: the belief that natural objects (for example, trees, mountains, natural phenomena and the universe itself) possess souls. Page 107.

anti-imperialist: against or opposed to imperialism. *Imperialism* is the policy or action by which one country controls another country or territory. Most such control is achieved by military means to gain economic and political advantages. Page 86.

approximity: fact, condition or position of being near or close by. Page 77.

Apra Harbor: a harbor on the western coast of the island of Guam in the northwestern Pacific Ocean. Apra Harbor is the best location on the island to anchor ships. Page 38.

archie: slang for an antiaircraft gun. Page 48.

arid: having little rain; very dry. Page 13.

armament: the weapons of a group of soldiers. Page 89.

Asiatic Station(s): a *station* (in full, *naval station*) is a place (such as a port or harbor) or a region to which a naval ship or fleet is assigned for duty. *Asiatic Station* refers to any such place located in Asia, for example, Guam, Hong Kong, Manila, Shanghai, etc. Page 25.

A.T.C.: an abbreviation for *Air Transport Command,* an organization within the United States Army Air Forces (the predecessor of the US Air Force) that developed a worldwide system of military air transport starting with the United States' involvement in World War II (1939–1945). The organization was charged with ferrying all aircraft within the US and to destinations overseas as well as transportation by air of personnel, materiel and mail for all war deliveries. Page 11.

aura: a subtle quality, atmosphere, force or field seen as surrounding or emanating from a person. Page 109.

B

baling wire: a reference to wire used to tie bales together. A *bale* is a large package or bundle prepared for storage, shipping or sale, especially one tightly compressed and secured by wires, hoops, cords, etc. Page 39.

banana interests: financial investments in small, politically unstable states or countries, usually in Central America, that are dependent on foreign funds to support their fruit-exporting economy. Page 86.

bandoleer(s): a broad belt worn over the shoulder by soldiers and having a number of small loops or pockets, for holding ammunition. Page 89.

barbarism: an absence of culture; uncivilized ignorance marked by wild, violent cruelty. Page 74.

barnstorming: in the early days of aviation, touring (the country) giving short airplane rides, exhibitions of stunt flying, etc. This term comes from the use of barns as hangars. Page 86.

barometer: a device that measures the weight or pressure of the atmosphere, thus judging probable changes in the weather. A barometer that is dropping shows that the air pressure is dropping and so signals worsening weather. Page 67.

barracuda: any of a family of marine fish with long, slender bodies and forked tail fins. Barracudas have large jaws and sharp teeth. They feed mainly on other fish but sometimes attack people. A barracuda can grow to about 6 feet (1.8 meters) and 100 pounds (45 kilograms). The largest variety, the great barracuda, can reach lengths of up to 10 feet (3 meters). It is called the "tiger of the sea" because it is swift and destructive. Page 45.

basement band: a group of amateur musicians that practices or performs in a *basement,* the part of a building that is wholly or partly below ground level. Page 53.

bass horn: *bass* means low or deep in sound. A *bass horn* is a wind instrument (a musical instrument sounded by wind, especially by the breath) of the lowest pitch. Page 69.

battened down: a nautical term meaning secured or fastened down with a *batten,* a thin, flat length of wood or metal used for various purposes, such as to hold a tarpaulin (a heavy-duty waterproof cloth) over a hatch to keep the water out. Page 67.

battle flag: literally, a flag that leads troops into battle. Used figuratively for any cloth having a distinctive design or emblem. Page 93.

bawled (someone) out: reprimanded or scolded (someone) loudly or severely. Page 44.

bearings, took (one's): determined one's position with regard to surrounding objects. Page 34.

beckoning: extending interest or attraction (to someone or something); tempting. Page 77.

bedrock: the solid rock beneath a layer of soil, rock fragments or gravel. Page 95.

bent: determined; set; strongly inclined. Page 5.

beset: plagued or troubled. Page 20.

betel nut: the dark red seed of a type of palm tree, wrapped in betel leaf and chewed in Asian areas as a mild stimulant. Page 37.

billet: a lodging place or a place assigned as a bunk, berth, etc. Page 93.

Billy Dollar: a small passenger vessel owned by the Dollar Steamship Company. Page 31.

bivouacked: settled, as by making a casual or temporary stay in a place. Page 93.

blackjack: a gambling game at cards in which any player wins who gets cards totaling twenty-one points or less while the dealer gets either a smaller total or a total exceeding twenty-one points. Also called *twenty-one.* Page 98.

black sand: a dark-colored sand having a high concentration of heavy minerals such as iron. Black sand can also contain gold, since gold is also heavy, but separating the tiny particles of gold from the black sand is a time-consuming process. Page 98.

blat: a senseless or disorderly noise. Page 38.

bleakly: in a manner that is gloomy, sad, not cheerful. Page 77.

bleary: dim or blurred, as the eyes are, from lack of sleep or weariness. Page 27.

blockhouse: a small fort or building with loopholes (small slits or holes in a wall) to shoot from. Page 77.

bluebird(s): an American songbird, the male of which has a blue head, back and wings. Page 14.

blue, done in: decorated in blue color, as by writing, painting or the like. Page 73.

blues: a reference to one of the blue uniforms of the United States Navy. The navy has many types of uniforms, depending on various factors, including weather conditions. Page 44.

Blue Star: a reference to the British steamship company, *Blue Star Line,* a large twentieth-century shipping company that used a distinctive design of a five-pointed blue star on the stacks of their ships. Page 34.

boa constrictor: a snake of tropical America, noted for its large size and its ability to suffocate its prey by coiling around it. Page 3.

bow(s): a nautical term for the exterior of the forward end of a ship. Page 30.

brawn: muscular strength, as opposed to intellectual power, such as that used in manual labor or physical work. Page 45.

breech: the part of the barrel at the back of a gun or cannon, into which one loads the ammunition. Page 48.

breeze, shot the: engaged in light or casual conversation; chitchatted. Page 98.

Bremerton: a city in west Washington, a state in the northwest United States on the Pacific coast. Page 49.

bridge: an elevated platform built crosswise above the upper deck of a ship, with a clear view all around, from which a ship is normally navigated and from where all activities of the ship are controlled by the captain or officer of the watch. The bridge of a modern ship is normally totally enclosed by glass screens or windows to give protection from the weather. Page 43.

Briny Deep Boulevard: a made-up address. *Briny* means salty and is used to refer to the ocean. Hence *briny deep,* a deep part of the ocean. Page 84.

British Concession: the northern section of the city of Shanghai, China, from the mid-1800s to the 1940s. The British Concession was organized as a business and residential area for British official and commercial interests. *See also* **concession(s).** Page 31.

brunt, bear the: have the greater part or main load of as one's duty. Page 46.

brusqueness: the quality of being *brusque,* abrupt or blunt in manner. Page 88.

Bubbling Well Road: a well-known street in Shanghai, China, so called from a famous well dating from the third century. The road was later renamed as part of Nanjing Road, Shanghai's principal shopping district. Page 31.

buff: a yellowish-beige color. Page 40.

buffoonery: something amusing or silly, something characteristic of a *buffoon,* a person who amuses others by tricks, jokes, odd gestures, etc. Page 39.

Buick: a car built by the Buick Motor Division of General Motors Corporation (an American automobile manufacturer). Page 13.

Bund, the: a famous landmark in Shanghai, China, a boulevard along the river lined with parks and European-style buildings. Page 31.

bunion(s): a painful swelling of the big toe, often caused by walking with poorly fitted shoes, that can be painful to someone traveling on foot. Page 11.

bust, China or: an expression of determination to travel to China, no matter what it takes, or burst or break apart (bust) with the effort. Page 56.

butted: hit or pushed against (somebody or something) with the head or horns. Page 14.

byplays: actions or speech going on to the side while the main action proceeds. Page 108.

by way of: by means of; by the route of. Page 9.

C

cab: the covered compartment of a heavy vehicle or machine, such as a truck or locomotive, in which the operator or driver sits. Page 12.

calm(s): an area of the sea without wind and without rough motion that is still or nearly still, posing a difficulty in traveling by sailing vessel. Page 11.

camaraderie: a feeling of close friendship and trust among a particular group of people. Page 20.

Camp Parsons: a Boy Scout camp located in Washington State, in the northwestern United States. Page 43.

canned: prerecorded in a standard form for general use, rather than recorded for a specific broadcast or performance. Page 12.

cannibals: people who eat human flesh, the practice of which has been reported in different parts of the world, sometimes as part of a religious ceremony. Page 37.

Cape Charles and Cape Henry: two points of land that jut into the sea at the mouth of *Chesapeake Bay,* a large inlet of the Atlantic Ocean in Virginia and Maryland in the eastern US. The opening to the bay is 12 miles (19 kilometers) wide between Cape Charles to the north and Cape Henry to the south. Page 84.

Cap Haitien: a seaport on the north coast of Haiti and the site of a citadel (fortress) built by Haitian king Henri Christophe (1767–1820) in the early 1800s. Page 85.

capitol, state: the large domed building, completed in 1902, in Helena, Montana, where lawmakers meet and decide on laws for the state of Montana. Page 14.

capstan: a device used on a ship, consisting of an upright cylinder that rotates. As it turns around, the ropes or chains attached to it are wound up, either by hand or machine, so as to pull up anchors, lift weights, etc. Page 69.

Captain Blood: the main character of *Captain Blood—His Odyssey,* an adventure novel (1922) by Rafael Sabatini (1875–1950), English novelist and short-story writer, born in Italy. Captain Blood is an English doctor turned slave, then pirate. (An *odyssey* is a long series of wanderings or adventures, especially when filled with notable experiences, hardships, etc.) Page 55.

Caribbean: the islands and countries of the Caribbean Sea collectively. The Caribbean Sea is a part of the Atlantic Ocean bounded by Central America, the West Indies and South America. Page 5.

carnivore: an animal that eats other animals; a flesh-eating animal. Page 40.

Cascade Mountain range: a chain of mountains in the northwestern United States and southwestern Canada that lies about 100 to 150 miles (160 to 240 kilometers) inland from the Pacific coast. The name of the range refers to the numerous small, steep waterfalls (cascades) found in a section of the chain. The highest mountain in the Cascades is Mount Rainier, 14,410 feet (4,392 meters), located in west central Washington State. Page 20.

catapult: thrust somebody unexpectedly and suddenly into a particular situation. Page 3.

caustic: cutting or sarcastic; bitter or sharp. Page 65.

cavalrymen: in the past, soldiers who fought on horseback. Page 55.

celestial: of the finest or highest kind; heavenly. Page 28.

centavos: Mexican coins of small value. *See also* **Mex.** Page 30.

Chamorros: the native peoples of Guam and the Mariana Islands, in the western Pacific Ocean. Guam is the largest and southernmost of the Mariana Islands. The Mariana Islands extend north 1,565 miles (2,500 kilometers) from Guam almost to Japan. Page 36.

Chang-Tso-Lin: (1873–1928) Chinese military leader who seized supreme power in Manchuria (a region of northern China) in the early 1900s, his efforts being supported by the Japanese as part of their plans to control China. During the 1920s, Chang proclaimed himself dictator of all China with his capital at Beijing. Overthrown by Nationalist forces, he was murdered when his train was blown up as he left Beijing. Page 66.

chaps: 1. people; men or boys. Page 43.
2. makes something cracked by exposure to wind or cold. Page 77.

chastise: discipline, as by administering some form of punishment. Used figuratively. Page 55.

Chaumont: the USS *Chaumont,* a naval transport ship that carried personnel and supplies throughout the Pacific prior to World War II (1939–1945), eventually becoming a hospital ship (renamed *Samaritan*). In February 1927, the *Chaumont* transported several hundred US Marines to Shanghai, where they were stationed to protect American citizens and property. Page 44.

Chen Shek: Chiang Kai-shek (1887–1975), Chinese political and military leader who tried to unify China but was defeated (1949) by the Chinese Communists. Chiang then fled to Taiwan and established a government-in-exile there that he claimed to be the legitimate government of China. He presided over the government of Taiwan until his death in 1975. *See also* **three principles.** Page 66.

chewed the fat: talked together in a friendly, leisurely way; chatted at length. Page 87.

chief officer: the officer of a merchant vessel next in command beneath the captain. Also called first mate, chief mate, first officer, mate. Page 31.

chilblains: red, itchy swellings on the ears, fingers or toes, caused by exposure to damp and cold. Page 11.

chill room: a room that is kept at a moderately low temperature, used for storing perishable foods to preserve them. Page 43.

China or bust: an expression of determination to travel to China, no matter what it takes, or burst or break apart (bust) with the effort. Page 56.

chit: a note, bill or any small slip of paper with writing on it, especially a statement of money owed for food and drink. Page 88.

chow: an informal term for food. Page 43.

cirrus: clouds with a wispy, featherlike appearance. Cirrus clouds are composed of ice crystals and found at average levels of 5 miles (8 kilometers) above the Earth. Page 44.

Citadel de Christophe: also *Citadelle Laferrière,* a famous mountain fortress constructed on top of a 3,100-foot (1,000-meter) peak outside the city of Cap Haitien in Haiti. Built during the early 1800s by Haitian king Henri Christophe (1767–1820), it took thousands of slaves to construct the massive walls, which were many feet thick and between 100 to 200 feet (30.5 to 61 meters) high. The fortress was supposedly built to house fifteen thousand men with enough food and water to last for a year. Page 85.

citation: a mention of a soldier or a unit in an official report, usually for actions showing heroic bravery. Page 89.

civvies: an informal term for *civilian clothes,* ordinary clothing as distinguished from a uniform. Page 88.

clannishness: a quality of being united together by some common trait, characteristic or interest; inclined to stick together as a close-knit group or family. Page 20.

clenching: sharply tightening the muscles of. Page 29.

cocoon: of or characteristic of a *cocoon,* a cover or layer over something. From the literal idea of a *cocoon,* the covering of soft threads enclosing some insects during an early stage in their development. Page 29.

coin: literally, a piece of metal used as a form of money or valuable exchange; figuratively used to express something given, offered or put forth as an exchange, reward or benefit. Page 11.

collaborating: cooperating, usually willingly, with an enemy nation, especially with an enemy occupying one's country. Page 66.

colors flying: outward signs of victory, triumph, success, etc. *Colors* refers to the flag of a ship, army, etc., and *flying* means waving or fluttering. The term alludes to a triumphant ship or victorious army with its flags waving in the wind. Page 27.

Columbus: Christopher Columbus (1451–1506), Italian explorer. He was one of the early few who thought that the Earth was round and that if one traveled west, a passage to India would be found. (The passage east was blocked by Africa.) Contrary to other calculations of the distance around Earth (of twice the length), Columbus proposed a calculation that was the equivalent of crossing the Atlantic Ocean. He was given permission and funded by the Spanish monarchy to travel west, based on his calculation. He discovered the West Indies and the coasts of Central and South America but never did make it to India. Page 84.

commandant: an officer in command of a US Naval District. Page 56.

commandeer: officially take possession or control of for military purposes. Page 68.

concede: acknowledge as true or correct. Page 3.

concession(s): a grant of land or other property, especially from a government, in return for services rendered or proposed or for a particular use; specifically, an area of land granted to a foreign power in a Chinese port or other trading center and permitted certain rights, such as the right of local self-government. *See also* **British Concession** and **French Concession.** Page 31.

condenser: a piece of equipment in the engine room of a steamship by which the steam, after use in the main engines, was reconverted into water for use in the boilers (tank in which water is turned to steam, which then serves as a source of power). Page 46.

Confucius: (551–479? B.C.) the most influential and respected philosopher in Chinese history. From about 100 B.C. to the beginning of the twentieth century, the ideas of Confucius served as the single strongest influence on Chinese society. Confucius stressed the development of moral character and believed that society could be saved if it emphasized sincerity in personal and public conduct. Page 72.

Confucius, Book of: a reference to the *Lun yü,* the most sacred writings of the Confucian tradition, consisting of sayings and other philosophical passages of wisdom. Page 72.

Conquistadores: Spanish conquerors of Mexico and Peru in the sixteenth century. Page 92.

constellations: configurations of stars, usually named after some object, animal or mythological being that they supposedly suggest in outline. Page 46.

contraption: a construction that appears strange or unnecessarily complicated. Page 69.

coolie: an unskilled worker, especially formerly in China or India. Page 30.

coral: marine organisms that live in colonies and have an external skeleton. Hard deposits consisting of skeletons of coral can form ocean reefs, islands, etc. Page 45.

cordial: sincere and expressed in an enthusiastic way; warm and friendly. Page 45.

Corozal: a town in north central Puerto Rico. Page 93.

cosmology: a particular description or system of how the universe is structured, the forces that created it and the like. Page 107.

courtier: an attendant at a royal court. Page 69.

cracks: humorous or clever remarks used in a joking manner. Page 45.

craven: defeated or overcome (as by something more powerful). Page 77.

cream: the best, most desirable or choicest part of anything. Page 46.

crow's nest: on a ship, a platform or shelter for a lookout at or near the top of a mast. Page 46.

crumby: dirty and shabby in appearance. Page 31.

cumshaw: something given, as money or a gift, in thanks for performing a service. Page 33.

Custer: George Armstrong Custer (1839–1876), American soldier and general. He and his troops were killed in a battle with Sioux and Cheyenne warriors at the Little Bighorn River in southern Montana. Page 55.

customs: the government department that collects the duties (taxes) imposed by law on imported or, less commonly, exported goods. Page 30.

cypress: a type of tall, straight evergreen tree. Page 69.

D

Dago: a nickname for San Diego. *See also* **San Diego.** Page 14.

deadhead(s): one who rides in a vehicle (as a ship or plane) without paying for a ticket, for example, as an employee (of a ship, airline, bus or train) riding as a passenger to an assigned destination. Page 84.

"dead soldier": slang for an empty bottle of alcohol, especially beer. Page 39.

deck golf: a form of golf played with a golf club and golf ball on a small-scale course that has a wide variety of obstacles such as wooden alleys, tunnels, bridges, etc., through which the ball must be driven. Page 27.

defection: desertion from allegiance, loyalty, duty or the like. Page 99.

defray: pay or furnish all or part of (the costs, expenses, etc.). Page 101.

deities: gods or goddesses. Page 36.

delta: a nearly flat plain of soil formed at the mouth of a river. Often, though not necessarily, triangular and so called because its triangular shape resembles the Greek letter Δ (delta). Page 30.

demagogue: a person, especially a political leader, who gains power and popularity by arousing people's emotions and prejudices. Page 66.

Dempsey-Sharkey: two American boxers of the 1920s and 1930s, Jack Dempsey and Jack Sharkey. Page 45.

denizen: an inhabitant or occupant of a particular place. Page 73.

deplorable: wretched, very bad and unacceptable. Page 84.

depredations: acts of preying upon; robbery. Page 68.

derelict: a ship that is, or is about to be, left or deserted, as by the owner(s) or guardian(s). Page 45.

de rigueur: strictly required, as by current usage. Page 3.

destroyer(s): a fast, relatively small warship equipped for a defensive role against submarines and aircraft. Page 28.

Diamond Head: an extinct volcanic crater that is a famous landmark at the entrance to Honolulu Harbor on the island of Oahu in Hawaii. It became known as Diamond Head in the early nineteenth century when British sailors mistook some volcanic crystals for diamonds. Page 28.

Dianetics: Dianetics is a forerunner and substudy of Scientology. Dianetics means "through the mind" or "through the soul" (from Greek *dia*, through, and *nous*, mind or soul). It is a system of coordinated axioms which resolve problems concerning human behavior and psychosomatic illnesses. It combines a workable technique and a thoroughly validated method for increasing sanity, by erasing unwanted sensations and unpleasant emotions. Page 3.

discordant: not in harmony; clashing. Page 74.

discrepant: harsh-sounding, as when sounds are heard together that do not harmonize. Page 30.

disdain: a feeling that someone or something is unworthy of one's consideration or respect; haughty (arrogantly superior) disrespect or indifference. Page 11.

dispirited: characterized by lack of energy and enthusiasm; gloomy. Page 25.

Docteur: the French word for doctor. Page 56.

Dollar: the Dollar Steamship Company, one of the largest American shipping firms in the early twentieth century, founded by Robert Dollar (1844–1932). A number of the vessels of the Dollar

Steamship Company were named for presidents of the United States. *See also* ***President Madison.*** Page 30.

dough: a slang term for money. Page 98.

down the hatch: swallowed. *Hatch* is slang for *throat.* Page 87.

drab: dull; cheerless; lacking in spirit, brightness, etc. Page 9.

dresser: a piece of furniture with drawers for storing clothes, sometimes with a mirror on top. Page 98.

driving: falling or being blown very hard and forcefully. Page 67.

dropped: ended the use or services of. Page 43.

dub: dignify (give an impressive name to something unworthy of it) or give new character to by a name, title or description. Page 109.

duffle: short for *duffle bag,* a large, cylindrical bag, especially of canvas, for carrying personal belongings, originally used by military personnel. Page 96.

dunnage: personal baggage or belongings. Page 44.

dunno: a spelling of *don't know* representing an informal pronunciation. Page 88.

duped: deceived or cheated; made a dupe. A *dupe* is a person who allows himself to be deceived; one who is misled by false representations. Page 84.

Durant, Will: William (Will) James Durant (1885–1981), American historian and author of popular philosophy. In the mid-1920s, Durant wrote *The Story of Philosophy,* a book covering the lives and works of the world's greatest philosophers. Written so the average man could understand it, it sold millions of copies. Page 25.

E

earnest, in: in reality; with a purposeful or sincere intent. Page 40.

earshot: the distance within which sound is audible to somebody. Page 77.

Eastern Seaboard: the region in the eastern United States bordering on the Atlantic Ocean. Page 86.

edifice: a large, impressive or stately building or structure. Page 53.

elephant hat: a lightweight, cloth-covered helmet often worn in tropical countries, especially for protection from the sun. Page 33.

El Morro: a fortress overlooking San Juan Bay in Puerto Rico that was built by the Spanish in the sixteenth century to protect shipping lanes in the area. Page 96.

Empress Dowager: Tz'u-hsi (1835–1908), consort of Emperor Hsien-feng. After the emperor's death, Tz'u-hsi, one of the most powerful women in China's history, ruled the country for three decades. Page 69.

engineer: 1. one whose profession is the designing and constructing of public works such as bridges, roads, railways, etc. Page 1.
2. one who operates a *locomotive,* a large machine that pulls trains on railroad tracks, originally powered by steam engines. Page 11.
3. a person in charge of the engines of a ship. *Second engineer* refers to the lower of two engineers or the next to the highest of several engineers. Page 28.

enlisted material: the type of person who joins (enlists in) the United States armed services and who is not an officer. Page 90.

ensign: an *ensign* is an officer of the lowest rank in the United States Navy. The term *22nd ensign* is used humorously to emphasize someone of particularly low importance or standing. Page 46.

entanglements, barbed wire: barriers formed of stakes and barbed wire, used in Shanghai, China, in 1927 when fighting occurred in the city between Nationalist forces and Communist forces. The concessions, sections of the city that had been set aside for foreigners, were protected by such entanglements while fighting occurred in other parts of the city. Page 31.

especial: special; particular. Page 29.

espiritismo: a form of spiritualism involving magic and communication with the spirits of the dead along with traditional church rituals. Page 107.

etched: engraved, usually on or as if on metal. *Etching* is a procedure used to reproduce images with a technique whereby part of the metal surface is "eaten away" by acid, leaving an impression of the image that can then be reproduced. Page 76.

ethnological: of or having to do with the science that analyzes cultures, especially in regard to their historical development and the similarities and dissimilarities between them. Page 107.

exec: shortened form of *executive officer,* the officer second in command of a ship. Page 43.

exile: the state of being barred from one's home and being forced to stay in some other place. Page 72.

exotic: from or in another country, especially a tropical one, which seems exciting and unusual because it is a foreign country. Page 9.

eyeshot: the range over which the eye can see. Page 77.

F

fabled: celebrated in fables (stories about extraordinary events or incidents); legendary. Page 65.

fagged out: exhausted. Page 95.

family seat: a place where a family lives, often used in reference to a large house in the country; a residence. Page 9.

far-flung: extended far or to a great distance; remote. Page 9.

fates: the supposed forces, principles or powers that predetermine events, the results of which are unavoidable. The word comes from the belief in three Greek and Roman goddesses (the Fates) who were thought to control the course of human events. Page 102.

fathom(s): a unit of length equal to 6 feet (1.8 meters), used chiefly in nautical measurements. Page 45.

Fear: a horror novel written by L. Ron Hubbard, first published in 1940. In the book, a college professor, James Lowry, having publicly denied the existence of demons and devils, suddenly finds that he has lost four hours of his life. The book tells of his desperate search to find the lost hours and of his descent into a grim world of night without day, of strange figures, of graves and murder in cold blood. Page 107.

Ferry Building: a well-known building in San Francisco with a famous clock tower. It is a terminal for ferryboats that carry passengers between the city of San Francisco and other points along San Francisco Bay. Page 27.

fete: a festive celebration or entertainment. Page 38.

feudalism: a social and political system in which the land, worked by peasants who were bound to it, was held by low-ranking nobles in exchange for military and other services given to high-ranking nobles. Page 25.

fiend(s): a person who is extremely interested in some game, sport or other activity. Page 43.

Filipino: a native or inhabitant of the Philippine Islands. Page 43.

Film boat: a launch (small motorboat) specifically used for the shooting of photographic stills. Page 43.

fireroom: a room on a ship containing the boilers. A *boiler* is a large tank in which water is heated and stored, either as hot water or as steam, and used for generating power in the engine of the ship. Page 28.

firing steps: boards or ledges upon which soldiers stand when firing (shooting) guns. Page 38.

fit as a fiddle: in good form or condition. Page 27.

5-inch gun: a cannon mounted on a naval vessel having a measurement of 5 inches (12.7 centimeters) across the center of the mouth of the barrel. Page 44.

flapjacks: *pancakes,* thin flat cakes made by pouring batter onto a hot greased flat pan and cooking them on both sides. Page 14.

flaunt: 1. make an obvious show of something. Page 55.
2. ignore or treat with scorn. Page 77.

fleecy: like *fleece,* the coat of wool on a sheep, in being soft and light in appearance. Page 67.

fleeting: fading or vanishing; dying out. Page 109.

flit: move lightly and swiftly; dart away; flutter. Page 38.

float(s): a vehicle bearing an elaborate display usually in a parade or a procession. Page 55.

flyblown: shabby, dirty or disreputable. Literally, covered with flies' egg deposits. Page 3.

"flying boxcar": a large freight-carrying aircraft. A *boxcar* literally is a completely enclosed railroad car, used to transport freight. Page 11.

foiled: prevented from succeeding in something. Page 102.

Forbidden City: a walled section of Beijing, China, built in the fifteenth century, containing the palaces of former Chinese rulers. Page 69.

forbidding: unfriendly or threatening in appearance. Page 77.

foreboding: having a quality that suggests something bad or harmful is likely to happen. Page 1.

forlornly: in a way that is *forlorn,* deserted or abandoned and showing signs of neglect. Page 11.

fortuitous: bringing good fortune; lucky. Page 56.

fountain, (soda): a counter with equipment for making and serving sodas, ice cream, soft drinks, etc. Page 43.

four-pass highway: a four-lane highway having two lanes (passes) for traffic in each direction. Page 21.

Fourth of July: in the United States, a national holiday celebrating the anniversary of the adoption of the American Declaration of Independence in 1776, marked by parades, concerts and large public firework displays. Page 45.

French Concession: the western and southern sections of the city of Shanghai, China, from the mid-1800s to the 1940s. The first of the foreign concessions established in Shanghai, the French Concession was developed with European-style homes and streets for the French officials and business people living in Shanghai. *See also* **concession(s).** Page 31.

Frisco: short form of the name *San Francisco,* city in Northern California. Page 27.

frivolity: behavior or activities that are *frivolous,* characterized by lack of seriousness or sense. Page 65.

frivolous: characterized by lack of seriousness or sense. Page 34.

frontiersmen: men living on a frontier, especially in a newly pioneered territory of the United States. In early US history, frontiersmen were vital in the conquest of the land. Page 20.

Fujiyama: also called *Fuji,* a dormant volcano in central Japan, the highest mountain in the country at 12,395 feet (3,778 meters). Page 28.

full tilt: at full speed or with full force. Page 93.

futility: lack of usefulness or effectiveness; pointlessness. Page 107.

G

gab, gift of: a talent for speaking; fluency of speech. Page 45.

gale: a very strong wind. Page 14.

galley(s): 1. a low flat-built seagoing vessel, formerly in common use in the Mediterranean, propelled primarily by oars. Galleys in ancient times often had two banks of oars and, in some cases, three banks. Page 11.
2. a kitchen on board a ship. Page 28.

garb: a style of clothing, especially official or other distinctive clothing. Page 72.

garçon: a waiter in a French restaurant. Page 88.

garish: overly bright and showy. Page 95.

gats: slang for pistols or revolvers. Page 96.

gaudy: showy and elaborate. Page 39.

gee-nan: phonetic spelling of the Chinese city of Tsinan (also called *Jinan*). *See also* **Tsinan.** Page 68.

geisha girls: Japanese women trained as professional singers, dancers and companions for men. Page 29.

general court-martial: a military court having the authority to conduct a trial for any offense against military law and to impose severe sentences, such as dishonorable discharge or death when provided by law. (*Dishonorable discharge* is dismissal from the armed forces as punishment for a serious offense such as desertion.) Page 89.

general delivery: a mail-delivery service or a department of a post office that handles the delivery of mail at a post office window to persons who do not have any permanent street address or who for other reasons call for their mail without waiting for carrier service. Often used as an address. Page 93.

geodetic survey: *geodetic* means of or having to do with *geodesy,* the branch of mathematics that deals with the measuring or determining the shape, curve and dimensions of the Earth or the exact position and measurement of a large part of the Earth's surface. A *geodetic survey* is a land survey in which these measurements of the Earth's surface are taken into account. Page 45.

germ: that from which anything springs or may spring; a source or initial stage of something. Page 108.

ghastly: extremely unpleasant or bad; terrible. Page 18.

gift of gab: a talent for speaking; fluency of speech. Page 45.

gobs: slang for US Navy seamen. Page 44.

Golden Gate: a narrow waterway connecting the Bay of San Francisco with the Pacific Ocean. It is 5 miles (8 kilometers) long and narrows to 0.6 miles (1 kilometer) in width. (In 1937, the Golden Gate was crossed by a suspension bridge, the Golden Gate Bridge.) Page 27.

Gold Star: United States Navy cargo ship built in 1920. In the years before World War II, the *Gold Star* carried both cargo and passengers between various parts of Asia from her primary station in Guam. Page 34.

Grand Rapids: a city and important commercial and manufacturing center in southwestern Michigan, a state in the north central United States. Page 12.

greasy grab: a taking hold of as if with a grip that is *greasy,* covered with an oily substance. Also alluding to the slang meaning of *grease,* a *bribe,* money or some other incentive given to a person to do something, especially something dishonest or immoral. Page 19.

great cheese ghost: a nickname based on *cheese,* a slang term for one who is considered influential or important, as in the expression "big cheese," the boss. Page 37.

Great White Fleet: a fleet of American warships which, in 1907, went on a world cruise to show the various nations of the world that the United States was a great naval power. All of the ships were painted white, hence they were popularly called the *White Fleet* or the *Great White Fleet.* Page 10.

Greeley, Horace: (1811–1872) American journalist and newspaper editor who popularized the phrase "Go West, young man" in the *New York Tribune* newspaper. It was meant as advice to the unemployed of New York City, referring to the opportunities of the Western frontier of America. Page 55.

grievous: very bad or severe. Page 56.

grind: (of a device or mechanism) operate by having some part or parts continuously turn around and around. Page 11.

grub: a slang term for *food.* Page 34.

grueling: extremely tiring and demanding. Page 9.

Guam: an island in the northwestern Pacific Ocean, a territory of the United States and site of US air and naval bases. Page 5.

Guantánamo Bay: an inlet of the Caribbean Sea on the southeastern coast of Cuba. Guantánamo Bay has been the site of a United States naval base since 1903. Page 83.

guards, to the: to the maximum extent or degree; completely; fully. Page 44.

guidon: a small flag, broad at one end and pointed or forked at the other end, originally carried by the military for identification. Used figuratively. Page 1.

gunner's mate: in the United States Navy the person responsible for the care and maintenance of a ship's weapons and ammunition. Page 48.

guts, rotting (one's): destroying the stomach, the intestines, etc., as by drinking excessive amounts of alcohol. Page 90.

H

hacienda grande: a Spanish phrase meaning a large house, as on a ranch. Page 100.

hailed: shouted or called at loudly to get the attention of. Page 87.

hairpin(s): a U-shaped piece of metal wire used to hold the hair in place. Page 29.

hair, within a: to a very fine degree, or down to the smallest detail. This phrase alludes to the width of a hair, which is very small. Page 100.

Haiti: a country occupying the western third of the island of Hispaniola (lying southeast of Cuba and west of Puerto Rico) in the northern Caribbean. Page 5.

hale and hearty: strong and healthy. Page 28.

hamlet: a group of houses or a small village in the country. Page 30.

Hangzhou: an important port and manufacturing center in eastern China. Founded in the early 600s, Hangzhou was the capital of China during the 1100s. Page 25.

hard-pressed: under a lot of pressure and without sufficient resources. Page 42.

hatch, down the: swallowed. *Hatch* is slang for *throat*. Page 87.

hatches: small openings in the deck of a boat leading to the lower level. *Battening down the hatches* involves fastening canvas over the hatches in preparing for a storm. Page 67.

Hawaii: a state of the United States since 1959, formerly a territory of the US (1900–1959). Hawaii is located in the northern Pacific Ocean about 2,400 miles (3,860 kilometers) southwest of the US mainland. It consists of eight main islands and more than one hundred smaller islands. Page 5.

haywire: in a disordered or confused state. Page 69.

heart, eating out (one's): also *eating (one's) heart out,* brooding about something that makes one feel unhappy. Page 89.

heel, bringing to (one's): putting (something) under (one's) control or discipline. From the literal sense of getting a dog to follow close behind one (at one's heel). Page 13.

heigh-ho: a phrase used typically to express boredom, weariness or sadness and sometimes to serve as a cry of encouragement. Page 100.

Helena: city and capital of Montana, a state in the northwestern United States bordering on Canada. Page 1.

Helena Independent: a daily newspaper printed and distributed in Helena, Montana. Founded in 1867, the newspaper is now called the *Independent Record*. Page 36.

helm, at the: literally, at the wheel or handle that controls the direction in which a ship or boat travels. Also used figuratively meaning at the place or post of control. Page 42.

Her Majesty's Secret Service: the branch of the British government that conducts secret investigations, especially investigations into the military strength of other nations. Page 65.

Herr: the German word for Mister. Page 56.

hitherto: up to this time; until now. Page 9.

hole, in the: in debt. Page 99.

Hollywood: a district in Los Angeles, California, well known as a center of the US television and motion picture industry. Page 12.

hombre: an informal term for a man. Page 43.

homestead: a dwelling with its land and adjoining buildings where a family makes its home. Page 13.

Hong Kong: meaning *fragrant harbor,* seaport and major commercial center, it is one of the world's largest natural harbors and is located on the south coast of China. A colony of Great Britain since 1842, it was returned to China in 1997. Page 25.

Honolulu: city in and capital of Hawaii, a state (formerly a territory) of the United States consisting of eight main islands in the northern Pacific Ocean. Honolulu is located on the island of Oahu and is the largest city in Hawaii and the major port and economic center of the state. Page 27.

hop: one stage of a long-distance journey. Page 34.

hopscotch, playing: moving by jumping from one position to another, likened to the children's game of *hopscotch,* in which a pattern of squares is marked on the ground and each child throws a stone into a square, then jumps on one leg along the empty squares to pick up the stone again. Page 100.

horses under his hand, thousands of steam: in control of a large amount of power (horsepower) from a steam engine. *Horse* refers to *horsepower*, a unit for measuring the power of an engine. The term dates from the early 1800s, when steam engines were compared to horses to determine a unit of measurement of steam power. One horsepower is equal to 550 pounds (249.5 kilograms) lifted to a height of 1 foot (30.48 centimeters) in 1 second. *"Thousands of steam horses"* refers to the tremendous amount of horsepower generated by steam engines, which were used to propel ships, railroad trains and the like particularly during the 1800s and well into the 1900s. *"Under his hand"* means controlled by, in reference to the work of an engineer. Page 11.

hoss: a spelling that represents an informal pronunciation of *horse*. Page 85.

hot cakes: another name for *pancakes*, thin, flat cakes made by pouring batter onto a hot greased flat pan and cooking them on both sides. Page 60.

houseboy: a boy employed to do cleaning and other domestic duties or general work around a house. Page 37.

H.P.: an abbreviation for *horsepower*, a unit for measuring the power of an engine. The term dates from the early 1800s, when steam engines were compared to horses to determine a unit of measurement of steam power. One horsepower is equal to 550 pounds (249.5 kilograms) lifted to a height of 1 foot (30.48 centimeters) in 1 second. Page 46.

Hubbard, Lt. H. R.: an abbreviation for Lieutenant Harry Ross Hubbard, father of L. Ron Hubbard. Page 68.

hubbub: confusion or uproar. Page 88.

I

ice plant: the complete equipment or apparatus for the manufacture of artificial ice. Page 46.

ifil: a medium-sized, slow-growing evergreen tree whose wood is known for its hardness and durability. Page 40.

illuminating: informative and enlightening, often by revealing or emphasizing facts that were previously unknown. Page vii.

imperial: of or having to do with an empire, emperor or empress, especially in reference to a characteristic color, design or the like. Page 73.

Indies: a shortened form of *West Indies*, a large group of islands between North America and South America in the North Atlantic. Page 18.

indigenous: originating in and characteristic of a particular region or country; native. Page 25.

Indonesian: of or pertaining to the people, customs, etc., of Indonesia, a country of Southeast Asia that consists of more than 13,000 islands, about half of which are inhabited. Page 36.

infused: filled (with something, such as a quality, feeling, etc.). Page 36.

Inland Sea: an arm of the Pacific Ocean, in southwest Japan. It contains hundreds of hilly, wooded islands that are notable for their fertile farmlands, copper mines and fishing. Page 29.

in lieu of: in place of; instead of. Page 38.

inscrutable: mysterious, unfathomable or not easily understood; incapable of being investigated or analyzed easily. Page 1.

insurrection: the act or an instance of open revolt against civil authority or a constituted government. Page 86.

INT.D.T.L.: the *International Date Line,* an imaginary North–South line through the Pacific Ocean, to the east of which the date is one day earlier than it is to the west. Page 45.

intermittent: used or worked on for a while, stopped and then resumed; alternately ceasing and beginning again. Page 65.

in toto: as a whole. Page 88.

isles: islands, especially small islands. Page 1.

J

jade: any of various hard greenish gems used in jewelry and artistic carvings. Page 33.

Japanese-backed: supported or assisted by Japanese forces, who had allied with local military leaders (warlords) in their attempts during the early 1900s to take over control of China. Page 66.

jeer: a rude, mocking (ridiculing) or taunting remark. Page 11.

jibaro: a person from a rural area of Puerto Rico. Page 107.

John: a slang term for the Chinese as a group or for a Chinese man. Page 73.

jolly: enjoyable; delightful. Page 33.

juke box(es): a coin-operated machine equipped with push buttons that automatically plays selected phonograph records. Page 11.

juncture: a particular point in time or in the development of events. Page 107.

junks: large Chinese boats, flat bottomed and high at the stern, with square sails held flat by thin strips of wood running across the sails. Page 30.

K

K.: an abbreviation for *kilometer,* a unit of measurement equal to 1,000 meters (approximately 0.62 miles). Page 68.

Kabuki: traditional Japanese popular drama, dating from the 1600s, with singing and dancing performed in a highly stylized manner. Page 29.

Kalispell: a city in northwestern Montana, a state in the northwestern United States. Page 13.

keeper: a person who has charge or oversight of a person. Page 55.

kerosene: a colorless, flammable oil, used as a fuel for heating and cooking and in lamps for lighting. Page 98.

keystroke: the pressing down of keys on a machine operated by a keyboard, such as a typewriter, thus activating them. Page 42.

kick: an informal term meaning to express discontent or displeasure; to complain. Page 46.

Kidd, Captain: William Kidd (1645?–1701), a famous Scottish-born pirate. In addition to attacking enemy ships, he also attacked ships of countries friendly to England. The English Government declared him a pirate, arrested him and hanged him for his actions. Page 55.

kidded: talked jokingly with someone in a light, playful way. Page 39.

kimono: a wide-sleeved robe, fastened at the waist with a wide sash, traditionally worn by Japanese men and women. Page 29.

Kipling: Rudyard Kipling (1865–1936), English author and poet, who wrote poems, novels and short stories set mostly in India and Burma (Myanmar) during the time of British rule. Page 11.

Kobe: one of the most important seaports in Japan, located in the southern part of the country. Kobe was founded in the 1100s. Page 25.

Kowloon: a seaport in southeast China opposite Hong Kong. Page 33.

Kranois: a fictitious lost city and people in Africa described by English author John Masefield (1878–1967) in his 1939 novel *Live and Kicking Ned.* Set in the eighteenth century, the story tells of an English doctor, Ned Mansell, who, unjustly executed for murder, is then returned to life. He leaves England for Africa, where he discovers the Kranois, whom he attempts to awaken to the danger of a threatened invasion. Page 11.

Kublai Khan: (1216–1294) the grandson of the founder of the Mongol dynasty, Genghis Khan. He completed the conquest of China begun by his grandfather. Page 65.

Kuomintang: also called *Nationalist,* the dominant political party of China from 1928 to 1949, which fought against the Communist Chinese forces for control of the country. *See also* **Nationalist.** Page 66.

L

lagoon: an area of shallow water separated from the sea by low sandy dunes. Page 44.

Lama Temple: a temple of *Lamaism* (also called *Tibetan Buddhism*), a form of Buddhism practiced traditionally in Tibet and Mongolia. It is characterized by elaborate ritual and belief in good and evil gods, demons, ancestral spirits, etc. One of the most prominent Lama temples in Beijing was built in the mid-1600s to commemorate the visit of the spiritual leader of Tibetan Buddhism. Page 69.

lamp: a slang term meaning to look at. Page 34.

large, at: as a whole; in general. Page 12.

late of: formerly but not now living in a specified place. Page 10.

latis: also spelled *lattes,* columns constructed of large stones by the ancient people of Guam, serving as monuments. Page 37.

latitude: the distance measured in degrees of angle of a point on the Earth's surface north or south of the equator. The North Pole is 90 degrees north; the South Pole is 90 degrees south. Latitude along with longitude is used to determine location. Page 19.

layover: a brief stop in the course of a journey, as to eat, sleep or visit friends; stopover. Page 88.

leaping: having the quality of being very startling to the eye or standing out, likened to something jumping out at one. Page 13.

leatherneck: a slang term for a US Marine, so called from the leather lining that was part of the collar of the Marine uniform. Page 1.

legation(s): the official local residence and office of a senior diplomat assigned to a country. Page 74.

lei(s): in Hawaii, a garland of flowers that is a symbol of affection, generally worn around the neck. Page 27.

Lesser Antilles: islands of the West Indies that extend in an arc from Puerto Rico to the northeastern coast of South America, including Dominica, Grenada, Saint Lucia, Saint Vincent, Martinique, Saint Kitts, Antigua and the Virgin Islands. Page 83.

lieu of, in: in place of; instead of. Page 38.

Lieut.: short for *Lieutenant,* an officer rank in the armed forces. Page 44.

light: fall or settle upon; land. Page 39.

lighter(s): a flat-bottomed open cargo boat or barge, used especially for taking goods to or from a larger vessel when it is being loaded or unloaded. Page 28.

lighthouse: a tower or other structure displaying or flashing a very bright light for the guidance of ships in avoiding dangerous areas, in following certain routes, etc. Page 11.

lime squeeze: a drink made of fresh lime and carbonated water. Page 33.

liners: large ships for passengers, mail, cargo, etc., especially ones on a regular route. Page 31.

lit out: an informal term meaning left a place in a hurry; departed fast. Page 39.

Lockheed: a US aircraft manufacturing company founded in the early 1900s. The company was well known for the design and sturdy construction of aircraft that enabled early pilots to set records for speed and distance. Page 12.

locks: the hair of the head. Page 39.

lolling: leaning in a relaxed or lazy manner. Page 74.

longitude: the distance measured in degrees of angle of a point on the Earth's surface east or west of a line that runs from the North Pole to the South Pole through Greenwich, England. A circle (the Earth) is 360 degrees—lines of longitude run from 0 (line through Greenwich) to 180 degrees east (E) and from 0 (line through Greenwich) to 180 degrees west (W). Longitude along with latitude is used to determine location. Page 19.

Luckies: a shortened name for *Lucky Strike,* one of the most popular brands of American cigarettes during the mid-twentieth century. Page 11.

M

main, in the: for the most part; mainly. Page 1.

malaria: an infectious disease transmitted by the bite of infected mosquitoes, common in hot countries and characterized by severe chills and fever. If not treated, it can cause death. Page 11.

Malay Peninsula: a peninsula in southeastern Asia, consisting of parts of the countries of Myanmar (formerly Burma), Malaysia and Thailand. Page 65.

mañana: the Spanish word for *tomorrow*. Page 100.

manganese: a hard, brittle, grayish-white metallic element, used chiefly in steel to give it toughness. Page 98.

mangy: figuratively, having many worn-out or bare spots. Page 93.

mania: excessive excitement or enthusiasm. Page 13.

Manila: a seaport in and capital of the Philippines. Page 34.

man-o'-war, Portuguese: an armed sailing ship or warship of the Portuguese Navy. Page 31.

Mao Zedong: (1893–1976) also spelled *Mao Tse-tung,* head of the Chinese Communist Party. Mao led the armies that won a civil war (ended 1949), transforming China into a tightly controlled Communist state, the People's Republic of China. Page 66.

martial law: the law imposed by military forces. Page 36.

Martinique: an island in the West Indies (a group of islands in the Atlantic between North and South America). It was colonized by French settlers after 1635. Page 83.

Masefield, John: (1878–1967) English poet, novelist, critic and playwright. Apprenticed as a seaman at the age of thirteen, he spent four years at sea, his experiences later influencing his poetry and fiction. He wrote more than one hundred books and was the official poet of England from 1930 until his death. Page 11.

Maxwell: the name of a popular and inexpensive automobile produced from 1904 through 1924 by the American car manufacturing company Maxwell-Chalmers and later absorbed by Chrysler Motors. Starting in the 1930s and throughout the next several decades, the Maxwell car gained fame as part of the comedy skits of American comedian Jack Benny (1894–1974). It became a running joke on Benny's radio and television programs that he was a miser who drove a Maxwell, which was characterized as an outdated, noisy, barely functioning car. Page 20.

medic: a doctor. Page 43.

mediocrity: the state or quality of being of only ordinary quality or being barely adequate. Page 12.

menu-broadcasters: a humorous term for those on board a ship suffering from *seasickness,* nausea, dizziness and vomiting resulting from the rocking or swaying motion of the ship. Not able to keep down the menu (food), they end up broadcasting it (casting or scattering it, often over the side of the ship). Page 27.

merchantman: a seagoing ship designed to carry goods, especially for international trade. Page 13.

merely: only what is being referred to and nothing more; just; simply. Page 3.

metacarpal(s): any of the bones in the human hand between the wrist and the fingers. Page 55.

Mex: coins from Mexico that were used in China (which did not have a national currency until 1933). Beginning in the nineteenth century, Mexican coinage was a key international currency, particularly used for trade. It consisted of silver pieces of several different sizes as well as coins of lesser value. Page 30.

middie: a shortened form of *midshipman,* literally, a student who is training to be a naval officer. Page 44.

midships: the middle part of a ship. Page 49.

"Mike," metal: also called *iron Mike,* a slang term for *auto(matic) pilot,* a control in the steering system, as of a boat or ship, that can be set to keep the vessel on a steady course. Page 28.

mile a minute: very fast. Page 93.

Milky Way: the spiral galaxy to which Earth and its solar system belong, some of which appears as a faint band of light in the night sky. A *galaxy* is a large, independent system of stars, typically containing millions to hundreds of billions of stars and isolated from similar systems by vast regions of space. Page 46.

milling: characterized by or filled with aimless or random motion, as of thoughts, actions, events or the like. Page 108.

mineralogical: having to do with the science or study of *minerals,* a substance that is naturally present in the earth and is not formed from animal or vegetable matter (for example, gold and salt). Page 1.

mineral rights: the ownership of the minerals under a given surface, with the right to dig them out of the ground and remove them. Page 83.

Moana: an area of Honolulu, Hawaii, near Waikiki Beach, in full *Ala Moana,* a popular park and beach since the early 1900s. Page 48.

moat: a deep and wide ditch surrounding a town, castle or other building, usually filled with water as a protection against assault. Page 73.

Model T: an automobile manufactured by the Ford Motor Company, the first motor vehicle successfully mass-produced on an assembly line. Model Ts were produced between 1908 and 1927. Page 10.

Mojave: a vast desert wasteland in southeastern California, covering about 25,000 square miles (64,700 square kilometers). Its flat, sandy stretches and dry lake beds are broken up by many small isolated mountain ranges and extinct volcanoes. Page 9.

moles: literally, small animals with dark gray fur, that are almost blind and dig tunnels under the ground to live in. Used figuratively. Page 108.

Mongolia: a nation in eastern Asia, bordered on the north by Russia and on the east, south and west by China. Page 77.

monologue: a long, uninterrupted speech by a single speaker, especially when being uttered by one person and dominating the conversation. Page 90.

monument(s): any enduring evidence or notable example of something. Page 65.

moon, shoot the: take something to the limit; go all the way, likened to hitting the Moon with an arrow, bullet, etc. Page 102.

moorings: places where boats or ships can be docked or secured. Page 30.

Morgan, Harry: also Henry Morgan (1635–1688), Welsh pirate who robbed Spain's Caribbean colonies during the late seventeenth century. Operating with the unofficial support of the English Government, he undermined Spanish authority in the West Indies. Page 55.

morrow: a literary term meaning tomorrow. Page 108.

mosaic: having pictures and decorative patterns made from minute pieces of glass, stone, tile or other hard substances of different colors. Page 33.

MPs: *military police,* soldiers who perform police duties in the armed forces. Page 88.

muchacha: a Spanish word meaning a young woman. Page 100.

mucho trabajo: a Spanish phrase meaning a lot of work. Page 100.

munitions: materials used in war, especially weapons and ammunition. Page 48.

myopic: lacking tolerance or understanding; narrow-minded. Page 66.

N

Nan-k'ou (Pass): an opening through the Nan-k'ou mountain range in China about 50 miles (80 kilometers) north of Beijing (formerly Peking). The pass is the site of a fortified section of China's Great Wall, well known as the site of battles against invading tribes. A railway, linking Beijing to areas in the north, runs through the pass and through a gateway in the Great Wall itself. Page 72.

National Guard: in the United States, the military forces of the individual states, which can be called into active service for emergencies, for national defense, as a police force or the like. Page 53.

Nationalist: of or supporting the *Nationalist Party,* a political party that controlled much of China in the early twentieth century, while fighting the Chinese Communists, who eventually gained control. Fighting was also going on with the Japanese, who had invaded parts of China during the early 1900s. In 1949, the Nationalists left mainland China for Taiwan and set up a government there that has continued to be separate from the People's Republic of China, the government on the mainland. Page 65.

nat'l gov't.: an abbreviation for *National Government,* the political body directing the affairs of China, at the time headed by Chiang Kai-shek. *See also* **Chen Shek.** Page 69.

Naval District: any of several geographical areas into which the United States is divided by the navy for purposes of administration. A Naval District is headed by a commanding officer who is responsible for the organization and effective operation of naval bases, recruiting stations, submarine bases, schools, navy shipbuilding activities, etc., within his district. Page 56.

nemesis: a bitter enemy, especially one who seems unbeatable. Page 95.

netted: acquired as a final result. Page 55.

Nevada: a state in the western part of the United States. Page 14.

newfangled: of a new kind or fashion. Page 11.

New Testament: the collection of the books of the Bible produced by the early Christian Church and covering the life and teachings of Jesus. Page 46.

Nicaragua: largest nation in Central America, on the Caribbean Sea and the Pacific Ocean. Nicaragua remained a minor part of the Spanish colonial empire until Central America gained independence in 1821. Since its designation as a republic in 1838, the country has had a turbulent history with frequent intervention by foreign powers. United States Marines were stationed there between 1912 and 1933 to impose order. Page 86.

nickel: an American or Canadian coin, made of the metals nickel and copper, that is equal to five cents. Page 33.

1917: the year that the United States entered World War I, which had been going on since 1914. The war was fought between the Allies (Britain, France, Russia and the United States after 1917) and the Central Powers (Germany, Austria and other European countries). Germany's military ambitions were largely responsible for the war, which resulted in its defeat in 1918. Page 13.

nipa bahai: a thatched hut. *Nipa* is a type of palm tree that grows in tropical parts of Asia and Australia, having large, feathery leaves that are woven together and used for roofing, baskets, mats and other such items. Page 39.

no-frills: relating to a kind of service or establishment that does not offer extra or special treatment; without any luxuries. Page 42.

none too: to no extent, in no way, not at all; used to emphasize that the quality mentioned is not present. Page 83.

Norfolk: a major seaport in southeastern Virginia, a state in the eastern United States. Page 80.

O

Oakland: a seaport in western California, on San Francisco Bay, opposite the city of San Francisco. Page 10.

oblivion: a state of being completely forgotten or unknown; destruction or extinction. Page 77.

Ocean of the Air: a term for the atmosphere of Earth, often with the idea of a region that birds, aircraft or the like can move through. *Ocean* here indicates an immense expanse. Page 13.

oil turbine(s): a type of ship engine that derives power from the burning of oil, which in turn heats water and creates steam that rotates one or more turbines (machines in which a liquid or gas acts on the blades of a rotor to produce rotational motion). The resultant rotation turns the ship's propellers and drives the ship through the water. Page 42.

oke: an informal term for *okay,* all right. Page 88.

Oklahoma: a state in the south central part of the United States. Page 13.

Olympic Mountains: a mountain range in northwestern Washington State. The highest peak is Mount Olympus, which is 7,965 feet (2,428 meters) tall. The lower slopes of the range are heavily forested, while the peaks contain many small glaciers. Page 14.

Olympics: *see* **Olympic Mountains.** Page 56.

onyx: a gemstone having alternating parallel layers of different colors, including white, brown and black. Page 101.

option: a right to buy something at a specified price within a set time. Page 100.

ordinary seaman: the lowest rank of sailor. Page 56.

Ore.: an abbreviation for *Oregon,* a state in the northwestern United States. Page 48.

Osaka: a seaport in southern Japan. Page 25.

outrigger: a type of canoe used in the South Pacific Ocean with a structure attached to it for stability and to prevent the canoe from overturning. The structure usually consists of a boat-shaped block of wood or bamboo, laid parallel to the length of the canoe and joined to it at each end by long bamboo poles. Page 36.

P

padre: father, used as the title of a priest in Italy, Spain, Portugal and Latin America. Page 95.

Palace Hotel: a six-story hotel on the Bund in Shanghai. Built in the early 1900s, the Palace Hotel was the finest hotel in the city. Page 31.

Pali: Nuuanu Pali, 1,200-foot-high (366-meter) cliffs on the Hawaiian island of Oahu. In 1795, Kamehameha the Great (1758?–1819) conquered the island when his troops defeated Oahu warriors, who fell to their deaths from Nuuanu Pali. Kamehameha eventually unified all the islands (1810), becoming the first king of Hawaii. Page 27.

pan: an open container for washing out gold, tin, etc., from gravel or the like, in mining. Page 95.

Panama: a country situated at the narrowest point in Central America. It is the location of the *Panama Canal,* a large waterway more than 50 miles (82 kilometers) long that cuts through the country, enabling ships to travel between the Atlantic and Pacific Oceans. Page 18.

papoose fashion: strapped into a device for carrying on one's back, similar to the method used in some Native North American cultures, where the baby (papoose) was often strapped to a board that the mother could carry on her back. Page 28.

Paris of the Orient: a name given to the city of Shanghai, the sophisticated commercial center of China, particularly in reference to its international atmosphere, which combines Western and Eastern styles of architecture. Page 31.

patrimony: anything inherited, as a characteristic or tendency. Page 11.

pay, out (one's): *out* means having lost money. Hence *out (one's) pay,* no longer having (one's) pay because of losing a bet. Page 45.

Pearl Harbor Navy Yard: the navy-owned shipyard (place where warships were repaired) at *Pearl Harbor,* a harbor in Hawaii and the site of a major United States naval base. Page 47.

pea soup: an informal phrase for a dense fog. Literally, a thick soup made of cooked, dried green peas. Page 84.

peeved: annoyed; irritated. Page 87.

Peking: (also spelled *Pekin*) former name of *Beijing,* a city in northern China, the capital since 1949 and the center of government in the country on and off for more than two thousand years. When Chiang Kai-shek came to power and formed the National Government (1928), he moved the capital to Nanjing, a city in east central China. Nanjing served as the capital until 1937 and again for a few years during the late 1940s. *See also* **Chen Shek** and **nat'l gov't.** Page 62.

penned: wrote with, or as if with, a pen. Page 53.

pennon: a long narrow flag, usually triangular, tapering or divided at the end, originally carried on a lance (a long weapon with a wooden shaft and a pointed metal head) by a medieval knight. Also, a similar shaped flag flown on the masts of ships for identification and signaling. Page 108.

people, (one's): members of (one's) family. Page 13.

perchance: perhaps; possibly. Page 20.

perched: set or placed on the top or edge of something. Page 84.

pergola: a frame structure consisting of columns or posts with a latticework roof, designed to support climbing plants. Page 33.

perilous: very dangerous; involving exposure to very great danger. Page 5.

period: the point of completion of any round of time or course of action or duration; termination, conclusion, end. Page 55.

perpendicular: extremely steep. Page 44.

Philippines: a country occupying a group of approximately 7,100 islands (Philippine Islands) in the southwestern Pacific Ocean off the southeast coast of Asia. Page 37.

philosophy: the love, study or pursuit of wisdom, or of knowledge of things and their causes, whether theoretical or practical; the study of the truths or principles underlying all knowledge, being (reality) or conduct. From Greek *philos,* loving, and *sophia,* learning. Page 3.

picturesque: visually pleasing enough to be the subject of a painting or photograph. Page 29.

pilot biscuit: a hard, saltless biscuit, formerly much used aboard ships and for army rations. Page 98.

Pilot Docker: a person who directs the tugboats (sturdily built, powerful boats designed for towing or pushing ships, etc.) that assist ships while docking and pull them away from the dock when departing. Page 43.

pinnacle: the highest point of anything, something that projects out or above others. Page 77.

pirated from: taken from (a place), as for one's own use. Page 19.

pitch: an alternating dip and rise of the bow and stern of a ship. Page 27.

pith helmet: a lightweight helmet or sun hat, originally made of the dried pith (inner parts of stems) of a plant from India and covered with cloth. Pith helmets are often worn in hot climates to protect the head, face and the back of the neck from strong sunlight. Page 3.

Piti: a town and port in southwestern Guam (a territory of the United States) in the northwest Pacific Ocean. Page 43.

plaintive: expressing sorrow; mournful sounding. Page 39.

plates: in ship construction, steel sheets that form the sides and decks of the ship. Page 28.

plight: a condition, state or situation, especially an unfavorable or unfortunate one. Page 19.

plug: a covering that is removed from a projectile and replaced by a fuse (a device that triggers an exploding device) before firing. Page 48.

plumb: completely or utterly. Page 84.

plumed: decorated with a *plume,* a large feather or group of feathers worn on a hat. Page 19.

Plummer, Ives, Piano Jim, etc.: local Montana outlaws and historical figures from the 1800s. Page 55.

plying: running or traveling regularly over a fixed course or between certain places, said of ships and other vehicles. Page 29.

p/m., revs.: an abbreviation for *revolutions per minute,* a phrase that indicates how many times per minute something (such as a mechanical part) will go around in a circle. Page 46.

Poe, Edgar Allen: a Marine Lieutenant on board the USS *Nitro,* who had a name similar to that of American short-story writer, poet and critic Edgar Allan Poe (1809–1849), well known for the strange and bizarre atmosphere in many of his tales. Page 44.

point(s): any of the thirty-two individual divisions of the *compass rose,* a circle divided into thirty-two points (or 360 degrees) numbered clockwise from the north and printed on a chart or the like. Points are used for describing sailing directions, judging the wind direction or approximating bearings of distant objects at sea or ashore. Page 47.

poking around: looking about curiously or searching here and there. Page 44.

pomp: a display of great splendor and magnificence. Page 34.

porous: having many tiny openings through which water, air, etc., can pass. Page 46.

port: a small round window or opening in the side or other exterior part of a ship, for admitting light or air. Also called a *porthole.* Page 67.

port bow: a position in front and to the left. The *port bow* is the left-front section of a ship or boat. Page 46.

Port Huron: a city and port at the southern tip of Lake Huron in southeastern Michigan, a state in the north central United States. Page 88.

Portland: the largest city and a major center of industry and trade in Oregon, a state in the northwestern United States. Page 10.

port(s) of call: a harbor town or city where ships can visit during the course of a voyage. Page 25.

Port Townsend: a city in northwestern Washington State (on the west coast of the United States), located at the entrance to Puget Sound and 41 miles (66 kilometers) northwest of Seattle. Page 49.

powder house: a building for storing gunpowder (an explosive mixture used in guns). Page 38.

precarious: not securely held; likely to fall. Page 93.

precipice: a vertical or very steep face of rock, etc.; a cliff. Page 56.

presently: in the space of time that immediately follows; in a little while; after a short time. Page 77.

President Madison: a ship built in 1921, named after American president James Madison (1751–1836), on which LRH traveled with his mother in 1927 to Guam. The *President Madison* carried cargo and up to 852 passengers. Page 27.

President Pierce: a ship built in 1921, named after American president Franklin Pierce (1804–1869). Primarily engaged in voyages across the Pacific Ocean from the west coast of the United States, the *President Pierce* carried cargo and up to 874 passengers. Page 56.

primeval: of or relating to the earliest ages of the world or human history. Page 107.

principles, three: the Three Principles of the People as defined by Chinese revolutionary leader Sun Yat-sen (1866–1925) and which Chiang Kai-shek said he was continuing. These were the principles of nationalism, democracy (realized in stages) and livelihood (guaranteed through collectivization of land and industry). *See also* **Chen Shek.** Page 73.

prop.: an abbreviation for *propeller,* a device on a ship consisting typically of a revolving shaft with spiral blades. The propeller rotates and serves to propel the craft by the backward thrust of water. Page 46.

protectorship: the state of being protected or defended, used with reference to the status of *Puerto Rico,* an island in the Caribbean Sea associated with the United States and having self-government in local matters. Page 83.

pro-tem: a shortened form of *pro tempore,* a Latin phrase meaning for the time being or temporarily. Page 45.

provincial: having or showing the manners, viewpoints, etc., considered characteristic of unsophisticated inhabitants of a province (a country, territory, district or region). Page 53.

P.S.C.: an abbreviation for *Patrol Submarine Chaser,* a small, unarmored patrol vessel. Page 44.

Puerto Rico: a self-governing island in the northern Caribbean Sea, associated with the United States since its acquisition from Spain in 1898. Puerto Rico is located 1,000 miles (1,600 kilometers) southeast of Florida. Page 1.

Puget Sound: a long, narrow bay of the Pacific Ocean on the coast of Washington, a state in the northwestern United States. Page 1.

punch-drunk: dazed or stupefied, as if suffering from the condition of a boxer who has been hit in the head repeatedly. Page 100.

punt: a long narrow flat-bottomed boat with square ends, usually propelled with a pole. Page 44.

puny: of inferior size, strength or importance. Page 19.

purported: that has been stated to be true, when this might not be the case. Page 38.

puzzle box: something mysterious and fascinating, likened to a *puzzle box,* a handcrafted wooden box engineered so that its sides can be moved, but only in a specific way and in a precise sequence to trigger the locks and slide open the lid. The surfaces of these boxes are covered with intricate patterns of inlaid wood that serve to hide the mechanisms that lock the box. Page 53.

pyorrhea: inflammation of the gums with a loosening of the teeth and a discharge of pus from the tooth sockets. Page 38.

Q

quake: an earthquake. Page 28.

quarantine, passed: a reference to passing an inspection by a health official, who comes aboard the ship to establish the presence of communicable disease. Finding no such disease, the vessel has "passed quarantine" and proceeds to dock. (If anyone aboard an incoming vessel has a communicable disease, precautions are taken to prevent the spread of the disease into the country by requiring a period of detention or isolation.) Page 28.

quarter: provide a place for soldiers to live. Page 33.

quarterdeck: the rear part of the upper deck of a ship, usually reserved for officers. Page 48.

quartermaster: an officer in the military responsible for lodging, clothing, transportation, equipment, etc. Page 65.

quartet: a group of four people singing together. Page 27.

queer: strange or odd from a conventional viewpoint; unusually different. Page 29.

R

rack: shake (a thing) violently; strain. Page 90.

racked (one's) brain: put pressure upon the mind, brain, etc.; strained severely with or in mental effort. Page 87.

racket: loud and confused activity; noisy confusion. Page 30.

radiant: filled with bright light; shining. Page 67.

rail pass: a permit, ticket or order allowing one free transportation on a railroad. Page 65.

rally round: to come together for combined action. Page 88.

rampart(s): a defensive structure built around a fort, castle or the like, made of an earthen embankment, often topped by a stone wall for protecting soldiers from enemy fire. The Great Wall of China was built to defend China against attacks from other countries. The wall is 35 feet (11 meters) high and, in some parts, the top is 20 feet (6 meters) wide, allowing for soldiers to hide on top of the wall and defend it from invading troops. Page 76.

ramshackle: poorly maintained or constructed and seeming likely to fall apart or collapse. Page 100.

ranker: an officer who has risen from the ranks (previously served as a private). Page 90.

rapier: a small sword, especially of the eighteenth century, having a narrow blade and used for thrusting. Page 19.

rattan: a cane or thin flexible rod used for whipping. It is made from the stem of a *rattan,* a tall palm tree with long, slender, tough stems. Page 31.

raucous: sounding loud and harsh. Page 1.

reacclimatize: become accustomed again to a new climate or environment. Page 53.

reconnoiter: to make a preliminary survey or inspection of an area. Page 38.

rectory: the house in which a minister lives. Page 53.

recuperating: recovering from something, such as an illness, injury, exhaustion or the like. Page 48.

redoubtable: that is to be honored or respected due to superior qualities. Page 53.

reformation: improvement in form or quality; alteration to a better form; correction or removal of defects or errors. Page 5.

Remington: a typewriter manufactured by the Remington & Sons company of New York. Remington typewriters were first produced in the early 1870s. Page 42.

reminisce: talk or write about events remembered from the past. Page 77.

respite: a short period of rest or relief from something difficult or unpleasant. Page 9.

retrospective: an instance or the action of looking back over situations, events, etc., of the past. Page 9.

revs. p/m.: an abbreviation for *revolutions per minute,* a phrase that indicates how many times per minute something (such as a mechanical part) will go around in a circle. Page 46.

rhum: the French term for a type of *rum,* an alcoholic liquor traditionally made in the West Indies and in parts of Central and South America. *Rhum* is made from the juice of fresh sugar cane and is found mainly in French-speaking areas of the Caribbean, such as in Martinique and Haiti. In contrast, the predominant ingredient in rum is *molasses,* a thick syrup produced during the refining of sugar. Page 88.

rickshaw: a small, two-wheeled, cartlike passenger vehicle with a fold-down top, pulled by one person, formerly used widely in Japan and China. Page 29.

rigging: the system of ropes, chains, etc., used to support and control the masts and sails of a sailing vessel. Page 67.

right, in (one's) own: by reason of (one's own) quality, character, ability, etc.; in or of (oneself), as independent of other things. Page 10.

river devils: a reference to a Chinese superstition concerning evil spirits or devils that inhabit rivers, whereby such devils are believed to be able to travel only in straight lines. To escape, cut off or elude such devils, small boats on the river would travel in crooked lines. Page 31.

roadster: an earlier type of open automobile with a single seat for two or three persons, a fabric top and a luggage compartment or folding seat at the back. Page 53.

Rockefeller Foundation: a medical facility, the Rockefeller Medical Union, built in Beijing by the Rockefeller Foundation in the early 1900s. The Rockefeller Foundation, a philanthropic organization, was established (1913) by John D. Rockefeller (1839–1937), American industrialist who accumulated great wealth through the Standard Oil Company, which controlled almost all oil production, processing, marketing and transportation in the United States. Page 73.

Rocky Mountains: major mountain system of western North America, extending approximately 3,000 miles (4,800 kilometers) through the United States and Canada. The width of the system varies from 70 to 400 miles (110 to 650 kilometers) and the elevation from 5,000 feet (1,500 meters) to 14,433 feet (4,399 meters) at Mount Elbert, Colorado, the highest point in the Rockies. Page 5.

roll: the rocking of a ship from side to side. Page 27.

rolling stock: the wheeled vehicles of a railroad, including engines, freight cars and passenger cars. Page 68.

roll, shot a: took pictures with a camera, using an entire roll of film. A *roll* refers to photographic film turned into a cylindrical form by wrapping it around a spool and then encasing it before loading it into a camera. Page 43.

romance: a spirit or feeling of adventure, excitement and the potential for heroic achievement. Page 11.

"Romance is Dead": a reference to the poem "The King," written in the late 1800s by English author and poet Rudyard Kipling (1865–1936). With the repeated phrase "Farewell, Romance," the poem portrays people in different periods of history saying goodbye to romance because it passed away earlier. (*Romance* here means exciting and heroic deeds and adventures, usually in a historical or imaginary setting.) Page 11.

rouge: a red powder or cream used for coloring the lips or cheeks. Page 38.

routed out: caused to get out of bed. Page 44.

Royal Hawaiian Band: a band formed in 1836, dedicated to preserving Hawaiian musical culture. The only band in the United States with a royal tradition, it was founded by Hawaiian King Kamehameha III (1814–1854). Page 27.

rubberneck: a person, such as a sightseer or tourist, who stretches his neck or turns his head to gaze about in curiosity. Page 65.

rudder: a means of steering a boat or ship. Usually a *rudder* is a vertical blade or something comparable, positioned at the rear of a vessel. Turning the rudder from side to side changes the course. Page 30.

rustic: of or characteristic of life in the country; having a simplicity and charm that is considered typical of the countryside. Page 107.

S

sacrilegious: relating to or involving *sacrilege,* the disrespectful treatment of something others consider worthy of respect or reverence. Peking in the late 1920s was a scene of inhumanity where people were oppressed by disease, starvation and lack of engineering, hence circumstances the Western world would consider sacrilegious. Page 62.

sage: showing wisdom and good judgment. Page 40.

Saki: also spelled *sake,* a mildly alcoholic Japanese beverage made from rice. Page 29.

salt pork: pork preserved in salt, especially fatty pork from the back, side or belly of a hog. Page 27.

San Diego: also shortened to *Diego* or the nickname *Dago,* a commercial and industrial city in southwestern California, a large port noted for its numerous military and naval installations. The area was first sighted in the mid-1500s by Spanish explorers. In 1602 it was named for fifteenth-century Spanish monk San Diego de Alcalá. Page 5.

Sandino, Augusto César: (1893–1934) Nicaraguan rebel leader of the liberal movement. After years of fighting in the mountains of northern Nicaragua, he was assassinated by the forces of the opposition military dictatorship. Page 86.

San Germán: a town in the southwestern part of Puerto Rico. One of the earliest Spanish communities on the island, San Germán was founded in the early 1500s. Page 100.

San Juan: the principal seaport and capital of Puerto Rico. *See also* **Puerto Rico.** Page 83.

San Luis d'Apra: a fort built by the Spanish in the early 1700s to defend Apra Harbor, the main harbor of Guam. *See also* **Apra Harbor.** Page 38.

San Salvador: an island in the West Indies, long held to be the first land in the New World (the part of the Earth that includes North and South America) sighted by Christopher Columbus in 1492. Page 84.

Santo Domingo: capital and largest city of the Dominican Republic, a country founded by Spain in the 1500s and occupying the eastern part of the island of Hispaniola in the Caribbean Sea. Page 96.

sash: a strip of cloth tied around the waist. As a part of traditional Japanese clothing, the sash, called an *obi,* is wound around the waist over the main garment and tied at the back. Page 29.

sax: an informal name for a *saxophone,* a metal wind instrument used especially in jazz and dance music. Page 34.

scant: barely sufficient or adequate. Page 1.

schooner: a sailing ship with sails set lengthwise (fore and aft) and having from two to as many as seven masts. Page 65.

Scientology: Scientology is the study and handling of the spirit in relationship to itself, universes and other life. The term Scientology is taken from the Latin *scio,* which means "knowing in the fullest sense of the word," and the Greek word *logos,* meaning "study of." In itself the word means literally "knowing how to know." Page 3.

scorn: feeling with which someone openly views someone as low or worthless. Page 40.

scudded: moved quickly as if driven forward by the wind. Page 67.

scuppers: openings in the sides of a ship that allow water on the deck to drain overboard. Page 67.

Sears Roebuck: a reference to Sears, Roebuck and Company, an American general-merchandise business composed of a chain of retail stores and one of the world's largest mail-order houses, founded in 1893. Page 13.

Seattle: a city in west central Washington State in the northwestern US and a major seaport and commercial center. Page 18.

Second World War: also *World War II* (1939–1945), conflict involving every major power in the world. On one side were the Allies (chiefly Great Britain, the US and the Soviet Union) and on the other side Axis powers (Germany, Japan and Italy). The conflict resulted from the rise of militaristic regimes in Germany, Japan and Italy after World War I (1914–1918). It ended with the surrender of Germany on May 8, 1945, and of Japan on August 14, 1945. Page 9.

semester: a division constituting half of the regular academic year, lasting typically from 15 to 18 weeks. Page 53.

sentry: a soldier who is assigned to watch out for, and warn of, danger. Page 38.

seven days out of Guam…: a reference to having been traveling for seven days but gaining a day due to having passed the International Date Line. The *International Date Line* is an irregular North–South line drawn on a map of the Pacific Ocean. It marks the point where navigators change their date by one day on a transpacific voyage. East of the line is one day earlier than the west. To account for this at a certain point close to the middle of the Pacific, navigators going westward add a day to their calendars (for example, the day after August 6 would be August 8), and navigators going eastward drop a day from their calendars (for example, the day after August 6 would be August 6). Page 45.

shade: a little bit; slightly. Page 11.

shamble: a shuffling, awkward walk. Page 74.

Shanghai: a seaport and the largest city in China, located on the eastern coast of the country. Shanghai is a center of industry, trade and finance. Page 12.

Shasta Limited: a railroad train that traveled through parts of the Pacific Northwest and Northern California. Beginning operation in 1895, the train traveled through scenic country, most notably near *Mount Shasta,* an extinct Northern California volcano that rises to a height of 14,000 feet (4,300 meters). Page 56.

sheds light (upon, on): clarifies; clears up; helps to explain by providing further information. Page 1.

Shelter Rock: a massive rock located on a trail in the northeastern part of the Olympic Mountains, noted for its overhanging section that can provide shelter in a storm. *See also* **Olympic Mountains.** Page 56.

shiplap: an overlapping joint between two boards joined edge to edge. Page 93.

shock-headed: having a thick mass of hair. Page 37.

shoot the moon: take something to the limit; go all the way, likened to hitting the Moon with an arrow, bullet, etc. Page 102.

shore leave: time spent ashore by a sailor off duty. Page 48.

shore patrol: the military police organization of the United States Navy responsible for the conduct of sailors on land. This organization assists military personnel, protects them from harm and investigates accidents or offenses in which they may be involved. Page 87.

short of: excluding; without actually resorting to. Page 11.

shuffleboard: a game in which standing players shove or push wooden or plastic disks with a long shovel-like stick toward numbered scoring sections marked on a floor or deck. Page 27.

shy of: being not quite at the point of; just prior to. Page 3.

sick bay: the space on a ship or room in a military base, etc., used as a hospital or a place where medicines and first aid are available. Page 43.

signing aboard: writing one's name on (something) for the purposes of identification or authorization, specifically, in being hired as crew aboard (on) a ship. Page 65.

Sikh: a member of a religious group that broke away from Hinduism during the 1500s and advocated a belief in one God, also incorporating some aspects of Islam. Following persecution by their enemies, Sikhs in the 1600s and 1700s developed a strong military tradition. By the 1800s, hundreds of Sikh soldiers in the British armed services arrived in China, some forming part of the *Shanghai Military Police,* the police force charged with protecting the international community residing in the city of Shanghai. Page 31.

silica: a very common mineral substance. Used in the manufacture of glass, silica is a component of almost all rocks, forming 59 percent of the Earth's crust. Page 101.

Simmons: a brand name for beds and mattresses made by the Simmons Company of the United States. In the 1920s, Simmons developed and introduced the "Beautyrest" mattress, which became America's first popular innerspring mattress (one manufactured with springs inside the mattress instead of stuffing material). Page 11.

sinister: threatening misfortune or harm; unfavorable. Page 56.

6-80: a naval launch (large military motorboat). Page 34.

sketch book: a collection of writings of a more or less descriptive nature. Page 9.

skiddled: moved quickly and lightly. Page 47.

sluice: in mining, a long, sloping trough or the like, with grooves on the bottom, into which water is directed to separate gold from gravel or sand. Page 93.

small-pox: involving *smallpox,* a highly contagious, often fatal disease characterized by prolonged high fever, vomiting and widespread eruption of pimples that blister, produce pus and often leave scars when healed. The disease was transmitted through physical contact or by breathing the air near an infected person. When introduced to new lands by infected explorers, epidemics of smallpox killed large portions of native populations. Page 37.

smart: having a neat and well-cared-for appearance. Page 31.

snap: an informal term meaning an easy task. Page 67.

snappy: characterized by being lively, energetic and active. Page 31.

snatches: small parts or bits of something; fragments. Page 38.

sneer: feel or show contempt (for something). Hence *"Scared? I hope to sneer,"* meaning "I have only contempt for any idea that I was scared." Page 47.

sobering: making (a person) serious or thoughtful. Page 107.

sock: a hard blow. Page 88.

solitude: a quality of being quiet, far from where people live and having little human activity. Page 38.

something lost behind the ranges: a line in the poem "The Explorer" by English writer Rudyard Kipling (1865–1936). The poem chronicles the trek of an explorer who, after hearing a voice telling him, "Something hidden. Go and find it. Go and look behind the Ranges—Something lost behind the Ranges. Lost and waiting for you. Go!" leaves the comfort of civilization to ultimately discover flourishing, uncharted lands. Page 56.

Sound: a reference to *Puget Sound,* a long, narrow bay of the Pacific Ocean on the northwestern coast of the United States. Page 55.

Southern Cross: a constellation in the Southern Hemisphere containing four bright stars so situated that they depict the extremities of a cross. Page 46.

South Pacific: the region of the Pacific Ocean lying south of the equator, including its islands. It extends southward from the equator to Antarctica. Page 1.

Soviet-backed: supported or assisted by the government of the *Soviet Union,* the world's first and most powerful Communist country, which lasted from 1922 to 1991, when the Communist Party lost power. Page 66.

Spanish-American War: a war waged against Spain by the United States in 1898, for the purpose of liberating Cuba from Spanish rule. Page 36.

Spanish Main: the Caribbean Sea itself, or that part of it adjacent to the northern coast of South America, traveled during the sixteenth through eighteenth centuries by Spanish merchant ships that were often harassed by pirates. Page 55.

spar: any pole supporting or extending a sail of a ship. Page 45.

spot: a small quantity of drink or intoxicating liquor. Page 88.

spud: an informal term for a potato. Page 98.

squared: literally, multiplied a number by itself resulting in a much larger figure. Used figuratively to express the expansion of something many times over. Page 11.

S.S.: an abbreviation for *steamship*. Page 96.

stagnant: characterized by lack of development, advancement or progressive movement. Page 25.

Stars and Stripes: the national flag of the United States, consisting of thirteen horizontal stripes that are alternately red and white, representing the original states. In the upper left corner is a blue field containing white stars, representing all the states. From 1912 and during the early twentieth century, the field contained forty-eight stars. The forty-ninth and fiftieth stars were added in 1959 (Alaska) and 1960 (Hawaii). Page 30.

state capitol: the large domed building, completed in 1902, in Helena, Montana, where lawmakers meet and decide on laws for the state of Montana. Page 14.

stateroom: a private room on a ship. Page 84.

steamer: a large vessel propelled by one or more steam engines. Page 11.

stick close: be loyal (to someone), here used ironically. Page 99.

stitch: an informal term for the smallest item of clothing. Page 94.

stock: ancestral descent; ancestry, usually with reference to race, ethnic group, region, etc. Page 36.

stood on and off: alternately receded from and approached the land. Page 34.

stovepipe: a pipe used as a chimney for a fuel-burning stove, usually made of sheet steel formed into a tube. Page 14.

straggled: followed an irregular course. Page 77.

stuff: material, such as facts, information or experiences, which can be used in creating or making something. Page 1.

sub-base: the submarine base at Pearl Harbor. A *base* is a location or installation on which a military force relies for supplies or from which it initiates operations. Page 48.

sub(s): short for *submarine,* a watercraft or naval vessel designed to operate under water. Page 28.

Sukiyaki: a Japanese dish consisting of thin slices of beef or other meat, vegetables and noodles, often cooked quickly and over direct heat at the table. Page 29.

sullen: dark, unpleasant and depressing. Page 1.

sunfished: bucked and twisted, similar to a horse that is *sunfishing*, bringing the shoulders alternately nearly to the ground and raising them. While bucking this way, sunlight hits the horse's belly and such a horse was said to be sunning his belly (or sides). *Sunfish* is a name for various fishes that like to be exposed to the sun. Page 67.

sun helmet: a hat with a broad brim, worn in hot climates to protect the head from the rays of the Sun. Page 85.

Supercargo: an officer who is in charge of the cargo and commercial matters aboard a merchant ship. Page 13.

supposition: an idea or statement that someone believes or assumes to be true, although he may have no evidence for it. Page 69.

Swan: a constellation in the Northern Hemisphere, roughly forming a cross, with stars visible as if at the head, wingtips and tail of a swan. Page 46.

swirl: a whirling mass or motion, as of water, air or dust; a state of whirling confusion. Page 108.

syndicate: a group of individuals or organizations combined or making a joint effort to undertake some specific duty or transaction. Page 83.

T

Tacoma: a seaport on the west coast of the United States, in the state of Washington. Page 10.

Tadamona: also written *Taotao Mona* or *Taotaomona*, spirits of the ancient inhabitants believed to haunt the mountains and wild places in Guam. It is thought that if the Tadamona are offended, they can cause bad influences in a particular location or toward a particular person. Page 36.

tagged (one) around: accompanied or followed someone around closely, often without invitation. Page 55.

Taku Bar: a seaport in northeastern China, at the mouth of the Hai River. Taku Bar (also called *Tanggu*) is the port of the city of Tientsin, which itself lies on the Hai River about 30 miles (49 kilometers) inland. (The *Bar* in the name *Taku Bar* refers to the sandbar lying at the mouth of the harbor area.) *See also* **Tientsin.** Page 68.

talking picture: also called *talkie,* a term from the early 1900s describing a motion picture that includes sound, as distinct from a silent film. Page 12.

tangible: real or actual, rather than imaginary or visionary. Literally, capable of being touched or felt. Page 9.

tapestry: a heavy cloth woven with various patterns or scenes depicting a story, usually hung on walls for decoration and sometimes used to cover furniture. Also used figuratively. Page 33.

Teddy and Harold: Teddy and Harold Mayhew, the sons of the owner of a photography studio in Guam. LRH's experiences at the Mayhew studio are described in the *Photographer: Writing with Light* volume of the *L. Ron Hubbard Series*. Page 38.

teeming: full of, abounding with. Page 33.

temperate zone: the parts of the Earth having a climate with a range of temperatures within moderate (temperate) limits. The Temperate Zones lie between the tropics (regions near the equator that are generally hot all year) and the polar circles, with very cold temperatures for all or most of the year. Page 11.

tenaciously: in a way that is *tenacious,* characterized by keeping a firm hold on something. Page 11.

tennis shoe: a sports shoe with a rubber sole and a stitched canvas upper that laces over the top of the foot. Page 48.

Thanksgiving: Thanksgiving Day, celebrated in the United States on the fourth Thursday of November, to remember the feast held in 1621 by the colonists from England who had set up a settlement at Plymouth, in what is now southeastern Massachusetts. Native Americans had shown the colonists how to grow food and the feast gave thanks to God for plentiful crops and good health. The customary turkey dinner now served at Thanksgiving is a reminder of the wild turkeys served at that first Thanksgiving celebration. Page 96.

them there: a humorous way of saying *them* with emphasis. Page 11.

thence: from there; from that place. Page 83.

Thibet: also spelled *Tibet,* a land in south central Asia, which has been part of China since the 1950s. Before China took control, Tibet was traditionally a religious kingdom, with Buddhist monks having a strong voice in its rule. Tibet's religion is a branch of Buddhism that seeks to find release from the suffering of life and attain a state of complete happiness and peace. Page 11.

thousands of steam horses under his hand: in control of a large amount of power (horsepower) from a steam engine. *Horse* refers to *horsepower,* a unit for measuring the power of an engine. The term dates from the early 1800s, when steam engines were compared to horses to determine a unit of measurement of steam power. One horsepower is equal to 550 pounds (249.5 kilograms) lifted to a height of 1 foot (30.48 centimeters) in 1 second. *"Thousands of steam horses"* refers to the tremendous amount of horsepower generated by steam engines, which were used to propel ships, railroad trains and the like particularly during the 1800s and well into the 1900s. *"Under his hand"* means controlled by, in reference to the work of an engineer. Page 11.

Three Faces East: a silent action film produced in 1926. Set during World War I (1914–1918), most of the film takes place in London in the home of a high-ranking British diplomat and deals with espionage during wartime. Page 43.

three principles: the Three Principles of the People as defined by Chinese revolutionary leader Sun Yat-sen (1866–1925) and which Chiang Kai-shek said he was continuing. These were the principles of nationalism, democracy (realized in stages) and livelihood (guaranteed through collectivization of land and industry). *See also* **Chen Shek.** Page 73.

throttle: reduce the speed of an engine by closing off the flow of steam to the engine. Page 45.

thwarted: prevented something from succeeding in or accomplishing something. Page 14.

Tientsin: a city in northeast China, one of the most important commercial cities in that part of the country. Page 68.

tiffin: a light midday meal or snack. Page 33.

Tilden, Nebraska: a town in the northeastern part of Nebraska, a state in the central part of the United States. Page 13.

Timbuktu: a city in central Mali, a country in northwestern Africa on the southern edge of the Sahara Desert. Founded in the late eleventh century A.D., Timbuktu became a center of Islamic learning. The name of this city is often used in phrases to represent a place that is very far away. Page 87.

Time **magazine:** an American weekly newsmagazine, first published in 1923 in New York City, New York. Page 13.

tin-panny: sounding harsh, thin or clanging; noisy. Page 40.

Tommy (Atkins): a term for a typical British soldier. *Tommy* is short for *Thomas Atkins,* a fictitious name used from 1815 onwards on a sample form accompanying an official manual issued to all British army recruits. Page 31.

took (one's) bearings: determined one's position with regard to surrounding objects. Page 34.

torrents: rushing streams of water, as from an extremely heavy rainfall. Page 67.

tortured: twisted, as from the extreme pressure of the wind. Page 67.

tourist track: a line of travel or the usual course or route followed by *tourists,* those who are traveling, especially for pleasure. Page 65.

transport: a ship used for transporting soldiers, military stores, etc. Page 31.

Transport Dock: Pier 12, a dock in the northern part of the San Francisco waterfront, where ships carrying naval or military personnel and equipment were loaded and unloaded. Page 56.

"Trapper Nelson" backpack: a backpack designed in the 1920s, based on a type of backpack used by Alaskan Indians. Consisting of a sturdy wooden frame that supported a canvas sack, the "Trapper Nelson" became a traditional backpack for Boy Scouts and others on hiking trips. Page 56.

tropics, the: the hottest of five divisions of the surface of the Earth, situated around the equator and including Central America, the northern and central parts of South America, most of Africa, southern India, etc. Page 40.

trumped up: made up or invented. Page 13.

Tsinan: a city in eastern China, also called *Jinan.* It is an industrial and transportation center, noted for mineral springs and religious and historical sites. Page 68.

Tsinan affair: fighting in Tsinan between Japanese and Chinese forces during the spring of 1928. In an attempt to halt the Nationalist drive toward Beijing, which threatened Japanese control of parts of northern China, the Japanese sent troops to Tsinan, supposedly to protect the lives of Japanese civilians. However, the result of the fighting was another success for the Nationalist Chinese and the withdrawal of Japanese forces. *See also* **Nationalist.** Page 74.

Tsingtao: also spelled *Qingdao,* a port city, naval base and industrial center at the entrance to *Jiaozhou Bay,* a sheltered harbor in northeastern China. The city and surrounding areas were occupied by the Japanese between 1914 and 1922, and again during World War II (1939–1945). Page 68.

Tumon: a beach area, now a resort, on the west coast of the island of Guam. Page 27.

turned in: went to bed. Page 44.

turned up: came or arrived somewhere. Page 13.

Turner, Lana: (1920–1995) an elegant blonde American actress who became a well-known example of Hollywood glamour. Page 13.

turret: a circular tower projecting from a building, as of a castle or fortress, frequently beginning some distance above the ground. Page 38.

twelve thousand horses: *horse* refers to *horsepower,* a unit for measuring the power of an engine. The term dates from the early 1800s, when steam engines were compared to horses to determine a unit of measurement of steam power. One horsepower is equal to 550 pounds (249.5 kilograms) lifted to a height of 1 foot (30.48 centimeters) in 1 second. Hence *twelve thousand horses,* the specific amount of horsepower generated by the steam engines that propelled the *President Madison.* Page 28.

two-bit: inferior or unimportant. From the informal term *two bits,* meaning twenty-five cents (which is a quarter of a dollar). Page 95.

typhoon: a violent tropical storm of the western Pacific Ocean area and the China Sea. Page 9.

typhoon belt: a geographic region in the western Pacific Ocean area and the China Sea, distinguished by its violent tropical storms. Page 34.

U

Uke: short for *ukulele,* a small, four-stringed, guitarlike musical instrument. Page 34.

under weigh: also spelled *under way,* moving; advancing; making progress. The use of *weigh* is in reference to the phrase *weigh anchor,* which literally means raise the anchor (of a ship), as in preparation for moving. Page 45.

Underwood: a manual typewriter invented in the late 1800s that allowed the typist to see every letter as it was being typed. Page 42.

USN: an abbreviation for *United States Navy.* Page 68.

USS: an abbreviation for *United States Ship.* Page 1.

USS Kitkat: a nickname for the USS *Kittery.* Page 84.

USS *Kittery:* a United States Navy ship that operated between 1917 and 1933, carrying cargo and personnel between the US and ports in the Caribbean. Page 80.

V

veldt: in southern and eastern Africa, open grassy country with few bushes and almost no trees. Page 11.

verandah: a large, open porch, usually roofed and partly enclosed, as by a railing, often extending across the front and sides of a house. Page 96.

Vigilante Day: annual Helena, Montana, parade and celebration in early May re-creating scenes from local history. *Vigilantes* were volunteers who, in some lawless areas, protected a community from criminals. Page 55.

vintage: of a certain time that something was produced. Page 55.

virgin: in its original state, untouched or undisturbed. Page 56.

wagging: moving back and forth. Page 74.

Waikiki: a popular beach resort in Honolulu, Hawaii. Page 25.

Wake Island: a group of three tiny islands that enclose a shallow lagoon, located in the central Pacific Ocean. In the mid-1800s a ship was wrecked on the nearby reef, stranding the survivors for several weeks on the island, which has no fresh water. Some of the survivors reached Guam in an open boat, but those on a second boat were lost at sea. Hence the statement *"so we'd better write,"* that is, they should send a letter home in case they have a shipwreck. Wake Island is primarily important for its strategic location and is currently administered by the US military. Page 44.

wake of, in the: *wake* is the visible trail (of agitated and disturbed water) left by something, such as a ship, moving through water. Hence a condition left behind someone or something that has passed; following as a consequence. Page 65.

Wang Po: an earlier spelling of *Huang-p'u,* a river in eastern China. The Huang-p'u serves as the harbor of Shanghai, one of the largest ports in the world, linking the city to the East China Sea. Page 24.

warlord: a military leader, especially a powerful one, operating outside the control of the government. Warlords ruled various parts of China in the early and mid-twentieth century. Page 66.

Warrant(s): short for *warrant officer,* a person in the Navy who holds a certificate of appointment (called a *warrant*) and ranks below the commissioned officers. (Commissioned officers derive their authority from a document issued by the president of the United States, called a *commission*.) Page 44.

Washington (State): a state in the northwestern United States, on the Pacific coast and bordering with Canada to the north. Page 1.

watchtower: an observation tower on which a guard or lookout is stationed to keep watch, as for enemies. Page 77.

way, on (one's): on (one's) course, path or journey. Also used figuratively to mean in progress toward accomplishment. Page 13.

weathering: enduring and coming safely through (a storm). Page 9.

weighed anchor: raised the anchor of a ship before sailing away. Page 34.

western hills: a range of hills in China, situated northwest of Peking (former name of *Beijing*). The range is known for its many temples and has long been a religious retreat. *See also* **Peking.** Page 69.

Western Story: one of the longest-running western pulps (magazines featuring stories about the American West in the 1800s). It was published until the early 1950s. Page 47.

whaleboat: a long, narrow boat designed for quick turning and use in rough seas. It was originally used for hunting whales. Page 44.

wharves: structures built alongside or out into the water as a landing place for boats and ships, sometimes with a protective covering or enclosure. Page 30.

wheel: circle; move around in a circuit or spiral. Page 45.

white-spired: having on its roof a white *spire,* a structure that extends or tapers upward to a point. Page 53.

will (to): make the choice of; exercise the will (free determination, desire, deliberate intention or wish) to bring about something. Page 11.

windmills at which to tilt: imaginary opponents or injustices to fight against. An allusion to *Don Quixote,* the central character in a novel of the same name by Spanish novelist Miguel de Cervantes (1547–1616). Deciding to combat the world's injustices, Don Quixote dresses in armor and sets out to perform heroic deeds in defense of the helpless. In one part of the story, he imagines a windmill to be a giant, which he attacks in true knightly style by *tilting* at it, charging at it with his lance. Page 12.

wind-sheared: having been cut off (sheared) by being blown down through the force of the wind. Page 65.

winsome: charming in a sweet or innocent way. Page 100.

wistful: having or showing a feeling of vague or regretful longing. Page 9.

world: the human race; Mankind. Page 5.

worldly: of or relating to this world; associated with things or affairs that are material rather than spiritual. Page 11.

wrought: brought about or caused by. Page 95.

Y

Yangtze: also *Yangtze Kiang* (now *Chang Jiang,* meaning *long river*), the world's third-longest river. The river flows from the Tibetan plateau through central China to the East China Sea. Page 30.

Yellow River: the second-longest river in China (also called *Huang He*) which flows more than 3,395 miles (5,454 kilometers). The river has a yellowish appearance, hence its name. As the river is subject to severe flooding, the devastating effects of its floods earned the river the title "China's Sorrow." Page 1.

Yellow Sea: western arm of the Pacific Ocean, between China's east coast and Korea, so named because the waters along its banks are a yellow, muddy color, from the yellow earth carried along by rivers flowing to the sea. Page 30.

Yokohama: one of the largest cities and ports in Japan, located about twenty miles south of Tokyo on the western shore of Tokyo Bay. The city was gradually reconstructed after being almost completely destroyed in an earthquake that struck in 1923. Page 28.

INDEX

E

F

G

moving to, 13

"Old Brick," *see* **"Old Brick"**

restless days in, 5

Montana National Guard

photograph of L. Ron Hubbard, 52

music

canned, 12

N

Nan-k'ou Pass

LRH photographs of Great Wall of China, 76, 77

railroad and Great Wall of China, 72

see also **Great Wall of China**

National Geographic **magazine**

LRH photograph of Great Wall of China, 76

Nebraska

Ron born in Tilden, 13

Nechodama, Helen, 96

Nevada desert, 14

photograph of L. Ron Hubbard, 16–17

New Testament

reading clear through, 46

Nicaragua, 86, 89

nipa bahai, 39

Nitro

see **USS** *Nitro*

Nugget

photograph of L. Ron Hubbard, 55

student newspaper staff, 53

Nuuanu Pali, Honolulu, *see* **Pali**

O

Oakland, California

photographs

en route from Helena to Oakland, 13

LRH, grandfather and Liberty Bill, 10

Oklahoma, 13, 14

"Old Brick," 14, 19

photograph, 15

LRH in front of, 14

"Old Homestead," 14

Olympic Mountains, 14

hiking in, 56

LRH photograph, 50–51

Oregon

Portland

automotive adventure, 10, 13

Orient, 18, 25, 31

Osaka, Japan

slums of, 25

P

Pacific

crossing at age sixteen, 18

exploring exotic lands, 9

Palace Hotel

Shanghai, China, 31, 33

Pali

Hawaii, 27

photograph, 47

thousand feet straight down, 48

Panama

seen by Ron age twelve, 18

THE
L. RON HUBBARD
SERIES

"To really know life," L. Ron Hubbard wrote, "you've got to be part of life. You must get down and look, you must get into the nooks and crannies of existence. You have to rub elbows with all kinds and types of men before you can finally establish what he is."

Through his long and extraordinary journey to the founding of Dianetics and Scientology, Ron did just that. From his adventurous youth in a rough and tumble American West to his far-flung trek across a still mysterious Asia; from his two-decade search for the very essence of life to the triumph of Dianetics and Scientology—such are the stories recounted in the L. Ron Hubbard Biographical Publications.

Drawn from his own archival collection, this is Ron's life as he himself saw it. With each volume of the series focusing upon a separate field of endeavor, here are the compelling facts, figures, anecdotes and photographs from a life like no other.

Indeed, here is the life of a man who lived at least twenty lives in the space of one.

FOR FURTHER INFORMATION VISIT
www.lronhubbard.org

To order copies of *The L. Ron Hubbard Series*
or L. Ron Hubbard's Dianetics and
Scientology books and lectures, contact:

US and International

Bridge Publications, Inc.
5600 E. Olympic Blvd.
Commerce, California 90022 USA
www.bridgepub.com
Tel: (323) 888-6200
Toll-free: 1-800-722-1733

United Kingdom and Europe

New Era Publications
International ApS
Smedeland 20
2600 Glostrup, Denmark
www.newerapublications.com
Tel: (45) 33 73 66 66
Toll-free: 00-800-808-8-8008